Making the Most of an Allotment Garden

Making the Most of an Allotment Garden

KEN TUDOR

DAVID & CHARLES
Newton Abbot London North Pomfret (Vt)

Dedicated to my parents, and written in memory of my grandfather, Sid 'The Lodge' Davies

Illustrations by Jennifer Johnson

Tudor, Ken
Making the most of an allotment garden.
1. Working-men's gardens
I. Title
635 HD1519

ISBN 0-7153-8445-7

Photoset by Typesetters (Birmingham) Ltd,
and printed in Great Britain
by Billings Ltd, Worcester,
for David & Charles (Publishers) Limited
Brunel House Newton Abbot Devon

Published in the United States of America
by David & Charles Inc
North Pomfret Vermont 05053 USA

Contents

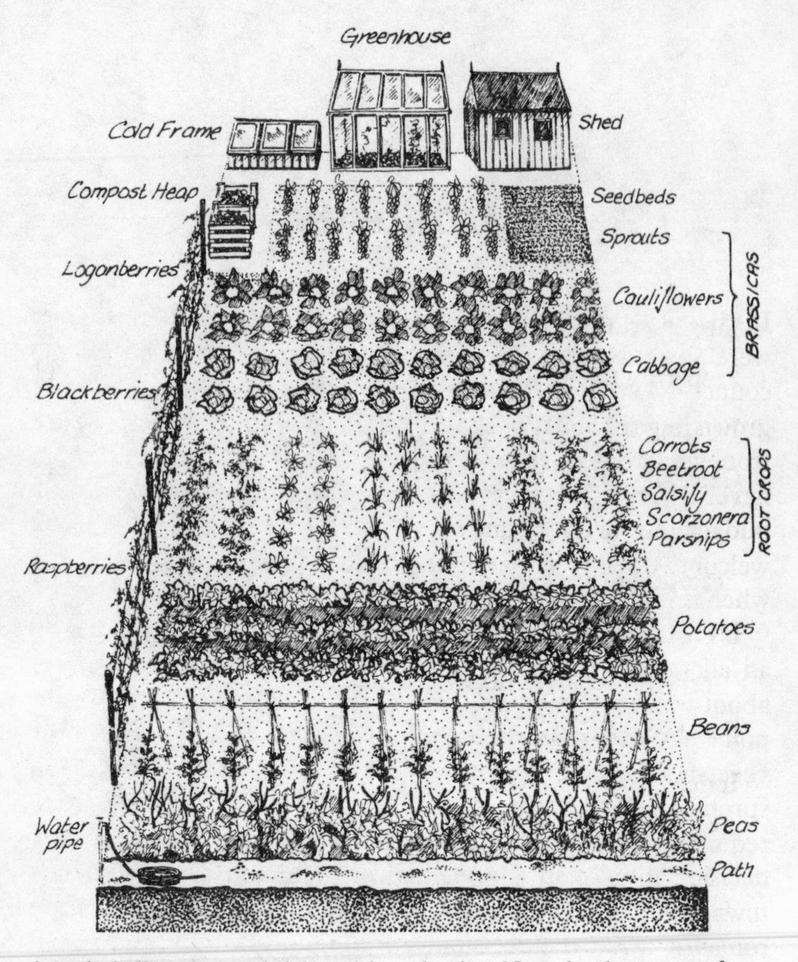

A typical allotment — thriving and productive. Note the short rows of root crops, for successional sowing across the plot

Introduction

In the 1930s men on allotments had a cloth cap image. They were working men who struggled on plots provided by the council to supplement a subsistence food supply with freshly grown vegetables. Today, nobody actually needs the produce from an allotment to be certain of a nutritious diet, but it can nevertheless make a very valuable contribution to the family budget throughout the year. The produce is particularly welcome when it arrives on the kitchen table in the winter, just when it is at its most expensive in the supermarket.

If I had to justify the twelve months' hard work demanded by an allotment to a doubting non-gardener, I would talk first about the satisfaction of working with the land. Then I would point out that when his family is paying sky-high prices for vegetables around Christmas, my wife and I will be picking sprouts, cabbage, leeks and broccoli, whenever they are required. These considerations played a large part in my decision to take an allotment in my adopted West Midlands town of Sandwell, but there was also more than a little romanticism in the decision, a feeling of returning to the soil and of escaping in the evenings and at weeks from the often suffocating world of competitive journalism.

It was probably this romanticism, this feeling of following my grandfather (a professional gardener) and my father (a keen vegetable grower) to the soil that led to those early rose-petalled dreams — a world of allotments crammed with vegetables requiring the minimum of work. I was to find, however, that there is one thing that all new allotment holders have in common, that plots are seemingly let to new holders only when they are hopelessly overgrown. My own plot, nestling amongst factories and urban sprawl in the Wednesbury area, was desolate and overgrown, a far cry from the dreams I had when I put my name on the waiting list.

The attempts to establish my plot into a working and productive garden were determined and difficult, leading to a period of considerable heart-searching and reappraisal. Did I really need all this sweaty, time-consuming effort, this blister-making release from the working world? My wife Linda set about the land alongside me, digging at the hard crust of a compressed clay-based soil, which was not unlike a dried-up river bed and which had to be punctured with the vigorous use of a pick-axe. Slowly, the subsoil, which in fact was only a few inches below the surface, was broken to the best of our joint efforts.

Despite these daunting hours of labour, our first growing efforts were frankly disastrous. This brought to us a curious mixture of emotions: much disappointment, some disillusionment and, of course, considerable embarrassment. How our neighbouring gardeners (now amongst our best friends) must have wondered about the cabbages that drowned in the sodden ground which had not been properly cultivated before the plants were transplanted too hurriedly! And how they must also have laughed (thankfully behind their vegetables) at the runner beans that refused steadfastly to climb my rickety climbing structure, and at the onions as big as marbles! Their amusement was understandable because this somewhat immodest journalist had chatted knowledgeably about the needs of plants and had told stories of growing in his native Wales, relating even how he used to help his grandfather grow mushrooms and peaches.

The gulf between theoretical knowledge, based on memories of working at one's grandfather's knee and a few glances at gardening magazines, and the practical dig-and-plant side of growing was all too evident in our first season. I realised, after a time, what the problem was. I had learned about transplanting and the care and storage of vegetables from my grandfather and my father who had been working with well-cultivated land. So we started again, not put off by the failures. In fact, we were spurred by our disappointments, and in our third year of cultivation real vegetables started to arrive on the dinner plates at home.

This determination to beat the substandard soil and to try to harness what nature offered to us had a marked effect on my life. It enriched my family life, it helped me to remain sane during a fiercely competitive regional newspaper battle, and it led me to a job as gardening correspondent, through which I have met and interviewed many of the country's leading growers.

The family involvement has been the big bonus. My wife now has a plot next to mine, my elder son grows flowers and vegetables and has almost two hundred cacti at home, and the younger son is never happier than when he has dirt all over his face and hands. In addition, there are the relationships with the gardeners on the other plots, a veritable kaleidoscope of the world, businessmen and labourers, unemployed and professional people, all striving to grow vegetables for their families and loving their own little piece of God's acre. Now, after more than twelve years of working together, there is a strong bond of friendship between us. We share our laughs, our sorrows over losses and our exaggerated predictions of the harvest to come. This bond, the family involvement, the therapy of hard work on a tired brain and the never-ending supply of tasty food has brought a rich seam of happiness to my life. It really is the good life!

1 Preparing the allotment

Every aspect of horticulture has its fascinations and challenges but there can be few more satisfying sensations than to pull fresh, young, healthy vegetables from an allotment garden at the end of a successful growing season. To take home from a once-overgrown plot a steady stream of varied vegetables gives a gardener a back-to-nature feeling that is important to many people in this age of high pressure living.

It is not always easy, however, to acquire an allotment from the local council, and you may have to spend several years on a waiting list. This is the result of the massive increase in the demand for allotments for 'grow-your-own' gardening which arose as food prices spiralled in the 1960s and 1970s.

During World War I there were about 1,350,000 plots under cultivation, and this was increased to over 1,700,000 in World War II. During the 1950s, though, the plots were used for development in many cities and towns, and at one time it was estimated that there were fewer than 350,000 plots in use for food production. Now there are over 500,000 in use and all allotment sites have long waiting lists of people anxious to get down to growing most of their own food. In the early 1900s a number of Allotment Acts were passed to consolidate the rights of plot holders. These acts give allotees the protection of a properly drawn-up tenancy agreement with the landlord, and this considerably reduces the chance of evictions for housing or industrial development.

Although there are still many private allotment sites throughout the country, local councils are responsible for the provision and maintenance of the majority of plots. Most councils offer tenancy agreements which strictly prohibit the selling of flowers or produce from the plots, insisting that allotments are provided only for the production of food or flowers for the allotee's family, relatives and friends.

To be placed on the waiting list for an allotment it is usually necessary to write to the local council's recreation and amenities department (in some areas it is the parks department) or to get in touch with the secretary of the site's allotment association. Sometimes the sites are run by the committee and they operate the waiting list, so it is always worth getting in touch with the secretary and showing an interest in the site. Sometimes it is possible to get involved in growing vegetables by helping someone incapacitated by illness or a grower who has been sent away from his home area on business.

The rent for a plot is very small; in fact, there are few areas where you will get such good value for money. A great number of plots are rented out at £2 or £3 a year, and this annual rental is rarely more than £10 to £15. A small outlay of £2 or £3 can be recovered by producing a good crop of cauliflowers at a time when they are at their most expensive in the shops or by having a plentiful supply of sprouts for the Christmas and New Year period. Cauliflowers, sprouts and the huge variety of vegetables that can be grown on the plot are not produced, though, without a considerable amount of labour. The plot needs digging, weeding, manuring and constant attention, especially in the main growing period between March and September.

During this busy period from spring through to autumn, the amount of time spent on the plot is crucial and will reflect the kind of harvest the garden will yield. It is, of course, impossible to lay down a timetable of hours needed for all the various stages of cultivation, but it has been estimated that to have a very neat and productive plot, with plenty of successional sowing and growing, it would be necessary to spend at least two hours a day on the land. I do not necessarily subscribe to this view, although if anyone has that sort of time to spare, it is almost certain that if he or she sticks to reasonably elementary garden rules, a regular supply of food will be available from the plot. Nevertheless, at least seven to ten hours of dedicated work per week are needed to run a plot properly. For example, the plot needs regular visits throughout the main growing season for sowing, planting, watering and feeding, as well as other chores like weeding and hoeing. For this reason the plot should be reasonably near to the grower's home, preferably within walking distance or a couple of minutes drive in the car.

In my experience there is often a high turnover of tenants on plots — confirming that it needs a combination of stamina, determination and will to win to run a plot year after year — but if the waiting lists on the council-run plots are long and slow to move, it is as well to remember that there are still some private landowners who have allotment sites. Some companies possess them on their works premises and large nationalised giants like British Rail and the National Coal Board have them on spare land around their depots.

Once the plot has been acquired, the gardener — often a complete newcomer to the world of vegetable growing — needs to gain a reasonable knowledge of the soil, of sowing and transplanting methods and the ways and means of providing nutrients to the plants. If he or she does not know much about the basics of growing, there are always books which can put the learner on the right track. Perhaps even more enlightening, however, are the older gardeners in the area, the experienced growers who have been working on the local soil for many years. A walk around the vegetable plot of an older gardener can educate a novice in a very short time, and he or she can learn which crops — especially potatoes, carrots and peas — are best suited to the particular soil conditions of the area.

There is a tremendous difference between growing on an allotment and cultivating the back garden of a house. It is mainly in the field of improvisation, the use of spare parts to make very cheap cloches, frames and sheds, that it shows. As the plot is used exclusively as a utility patch, with the production of food the only aim, the plot holder is not over-worried about neatness and does not have one eye on a critical neighbour. The allotment sheds, frames, fences and compost heaps can all be constructed from spares pieces of material —

Bedsteads can be propped up, and peas and beans trained up them — they are sturdy, rust-free and, if properly erected, wind resistant

old doors, windows, wooden pallets and old machine boxes. Then there are the stakes for tall-growing vegetables. On the allotment anything that will stick in the ground can be used to hold up peas, beans and any other vegetables requiring support — even bedsteads can be used. Kitchen gardeners often feel they have to buy manufactured compost bins, but on the plot there is room for any container. Old oil drums, properly washed with detergent, can be used, once holes have been knocked into the sides and bottom of the bin. Wire cages, made from pieces of old fencing, can also be used to hold compost.

Newcomers to an allotment are always fired by ambition to dig it as quickly as they can and to set out the garden in the shortest possible time. However, if I was to take over a new allotment tomorrow morning, I would set about doing one thing immediately — getting the paths and boundaries settled properly. For if there was one mistake I made in the early years of my allotment gardening, it was in wasting hundreds of hours repairing the path and boundaries, when the laying of secondhand slabs or bricks would have made the path a firm, permanent and easy-to-maintain walkway. Also make sure that there are boards or bricks around the boundary of the allotment plot so that there are no discussions, friendly or otherwise, with your neighbours about the exact position of the boundary. This also helps to ensure that one of the gardeners does not accidentally damage another plot holder's produce.

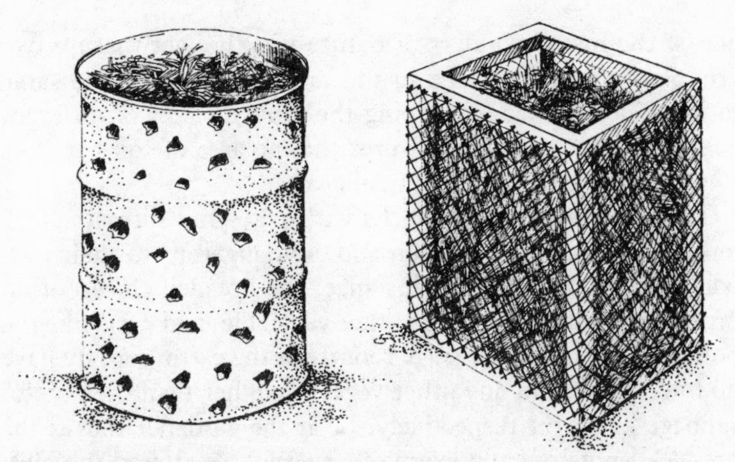

Almost anything can be used for storing compost — an old oil drum, with holes knocked into the sides and bottom, and wire fencing fixed in a square or circle

Crop rotation

Once the paths and boundaries have been laid out, the soil has been turned over and the perennial weeds removed, it is time to consider which plants to grow and in what quantities, and, most importantly, where on the plot they should be grown. The planning of the plot is one of the most important jobs of the year.

To grow successfully season after season, it is vital to operate a crop rotation scheme. Without a proper system of crop rotation, plants which are grown year after year in the same section of land look sick and become relatively unproductive as the balance of the plot's nutrients is lost. The allotment man or woman would be wise to follow the example of farmers and vegetable growers through the ages who found centuries ago that planting the same crops every season on the same strip of land soon became uneconomic and brought on many soil-borne pests and diseases. For years they left the fields fallow, believing that they were 'raping' the land and that resting it periodically would result in more economic harvests. A crop rotational system was introduced when it was discovered that one of the many wonders of nature was the fact that no two groups of vegetables take in the same nutrients in the same ratios. Therefore, by swapping the growing sites of different vegetables, the gardener ensures that no area of soil becomes 'sour' for any particular group of crops.

The same system also works with pests and diseases since most pests only prevail upon and are dangerous to their own particular host plant. For instance, the dreaded club root on brassicas does not affect any other vegetable, and pests like the potato eelworm, the cabbage root fly or the carrot root fly have no interest at all in any other vegetable other than the potato, cabbage or carrot respectively. So if the gardener moves the brassicas, potatoes and every other vegetable around the plot, the incidence of serious disease and pest damage can be considerably reduced if not completely eradicated.

The newcomer to gardening should also recognise that different types of vegetables have their own needs and special qualities. For example, members of the legume family, which includes peas, runner beans and dwarf beans, naturally produce nitrogen in the ground through highly efficient nodules on their root ends. If nature throws up such sophisticated plants, it is up to man to make use of them; so when the peas and beans have finished cropping, it is a good idea to cut down only the tops of the plants and leave the root systems in the ground for a week or so to deposit their nitrogen stores into the soil. Likewise, brassicas and leeks, which enjoy nitrogen and take up huge amounts of it from the soil structure, should be planted in newly cleared ground. It seems to me that nature was planning rotational schemes for crops centuries before the idea finally dawned on man!

Before working out what goes where in the plot, it is wise to draw up a simple plan of the garden, splitting its area into three equal sections. List also the crops that are to be grown dividing them into three groups as follows:

Plot A	Root crops	Carrots, beetroot, onions and parsnips

Plot B	Brassicas	Broccoli, cabbage, cauliflowers, spinach, sprouts, swedes and turnips
Plot C	Other crops	Broad beans, dwarf beans, runner beans, peas and potatoes

Some of the vegetables that most of us grow do not fall neatly into one of the three main vegetable groups. For instance, tomatoes, sweetcorn and marrows are not included in the above list but they benefit from deep cultivation and therefore love the manure and compost content of the group which includes potatoes, beans and peas. Other vegetables can be fitted in with their known requirements and where there is room. For example, lettuce like to grow quickly and continuously, so they enjoy land which has been manured for the current season.

Use your commonsense in working with the cropping scheme and the production of food can be increased considerably. There are other side benefits of the scheme, such as the liming of the ground. The whole plot usually needs to be limed every three years and so the liming of the brassica plot every year means that this aim is achieved in the rotational cycle.

The need for the scheme has been demonstrated very recently on my own plot. I used to move the majority of my crops around but I liked to keep my peas and beans at the back of the plot. The beans were not affected by this working practice because the trenches were dug out and refilled with manure, compost and other garden waste at the end of each season. The big peas, the Achievements and their tall-growing varieties, continued to grow successfully too, again because the trench system of supplying new soil was used, but the dwarf peas grown under normal conditions started to return smaller and smaller harvests. These failures pushed me into moving the rows around the plot within the crop rotation scheme, and soon the Little Marvela, Kelvedon Wonder and Onward varieties were producing their usual huge supply of tender young peas.

I work on a three-year crop rotation scheme because my allotment is long and narrow and is therefore easy to split into

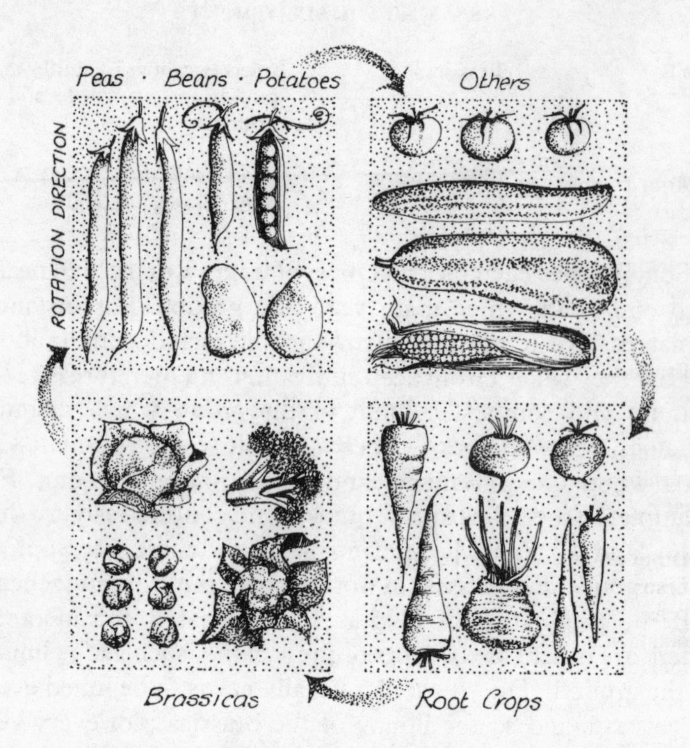

The four-year rotation cycle

three equal parts along its length. If, however, my allotment were wider I would rather run a four-year crop rotation scheme by dividing the plot by a central path down the length and another pathway across the middle. This gives four quarters which are easy to tend, weed, spray and work in a clockwise rotation scheme around the plot. The rotation system in use on my allotment is illustrated in table 1. The runner beans remain at the top of the patch each year.

In order to plan the garden for the greatest possible yields, it is worth considering turning the root plot so that rows of root crops run parallel with the paths on long allotments. This allows the gardener to sow short rows in successional sowing programmes which, if timed correctly, can yield small quantities of carrots and parsnips, beetroot and radish throughout the season.

Table 1 Four-year crop rotation scheme

Runner beans

<table>
<tr><td>Root crops
carrots
onions
parsnips
salsify
etc</td><td>Brassicas
broccoli
cabbage
cauliflowers
turnips
etc</td><td>Other crops
beans
peas
potatoes
tomatoes
etc</td><td>Root crops
carrots
onions
parsnips
salsify
etc</td></tr>
<tr><td>Brassicas
broccoli
cabbage
cauliflowers
turnips
etc</td><td>Other crops
beans
peas
potatoes
tomatoes
etc</td><td>Root crops
carrots
onions
parsnips
salsify
etc</td><td>Brassicas
broccoli
cabbage
cauliflowers
turnips
etc</td></tr>
<tr><td>Other crops
beans
peas
potatoes
tomatoes
etc</td><td>Root crops
carrots
onions
parsnips
salsify
etc</td><td>Brassicas
broccoli
cabbage
cauliflowers
turnips
etc</td><td>Other crops
beans
peas
potatoes
tomatoes
etc</td></tr>
<tr><td>First year</td><td>Second year</td><td>Third year</td><td>Fourth year</td></tr>
</table>

Crop selection

In the depths of winter, months before sowing and planting, I like to sit down with the family one evening and discuss what vegetables to grow. Most people will grow cabbage, sprouts, leeks, onions, runner beans, potatoes and carrots, and almost everyone likes to produce dwarf beans, beetroot, parsnips, lettuce and turnips. The only vegetables not on my list are turnips, simply because they are not liked in my own household. There are, though, other vegetables which my family love, for example, sweetcorn, courgettes and marrows.

When considering which vegetables to grow, it is important to consider how large the family is for which you are catering, and which varieties are suited to allotment growing and will produce an economic crop from the land used. For instance, for a family of two or three you should grow smaller vegetables, such as the small-headed Minicole cabbage. This variety of cabbage scores on the second point too, being absolutely ideal for growing on an allotment because it tolerates all weathers and can stand at maturity for several weeks which is especially useful to those who can only visit the allotment at weekends. Its compact growing habit also means that the Minicole can be grown closer together which adds to the productivity of the patch. It is worth considering Peer Gynt sprouts for the same reasons. This neat and compact plant produces beautifully uniform sprouts early in the season and, again, because of their size, they can be planted closer together than the taller sprout plants.

Most people like to grow potatoes to get those lovely tasty earlies on the plate with the spring lamb, but they do take up a lot of room. A number of growers I know only plant a couple of rows of earlies and buy the maincrops from professional growers. The land they save is then available for other more economic crops. It is also wise to include on the list a group of vegetables I refer to as the 'pick-and-pick-again brigade'. These include runner beans, dwarf beans, calabrese, broccoli, kale and courgettes. All of these vegetables produce more food if they are picked regularly, giving a prolonged harvest over several months.

Carrots are another must, not just because they are tasty and packed with vitamins, but also because of their long harvesting period. They can be sown in cloches, hot beds and cold frames from late January until late summer and will produce juicy roots from early June. The supply of carrots can continue through the winter because they can be successfully deep frozen, especially if pulled when finger-long, stored in boxes of sand and peat or simply left in the ground. I left two rows in the ground through the record frosts in the winter of 1982 and they were perfectly edible when the soil finally thawed in March.

Other varieties that can be picked throughout the winter must figure high in a top ten of vegetables, and these include winter cabbage, leeks, parsnips, sprouts and swedes. Then there is the salad crop — lettuce, radish, beetroot, spring onions and outdoor tomatoes. All these are essential crops for growers who are really determined to get the most from their allotment garden. The other banker crops are onions — seed onions, that grow large and juicy, sets that produce hard, good-keeping onions for the winter, and spring onions, the hot mini-bulbs used in salads.

Varieties of commonly grown vegetables

It is exceedingly difficult to suggest varieties for all parts of the country, but all the recommendations that follow would be worth experimenting with. It is in the interests of all gardeners to try as many seed strains as possible to see what grows best on his or her land.

Cabbage

The best cabbage in all the seed books, as far as my garden is concerned, is without doubt the Hispi. This is probably the most versatile of all cabbages; it can be sown in autumn and over-wintered in a cold frame for spring planting, or started in January or February for early pointed cabbages.

Another strong recommendation is the Minicole, already mentioned, for its ability to stand for up to three months

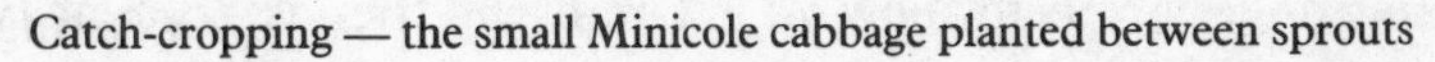

Catch-cropping — the small Minicole cabbage planted between sprouts

without spoiling. It is especially suitable for allotment growers because it can stand when visits to the allotment become infrequent during holidays or when other commitments intervene. It can also be used for catch-cropping between late sprouts which, because of their tall growing habit, have to be planted about 1m (3ft) apart. The Minicole cabbage can grow to maturity before the sprout reaches any size at all.

Celtic and January King are also recommended because they too can stand for long periods in the most inclement weather. This is important because they can be picked over a long period when vegetables are at their most expensive in the shops.

Carrots

Amsterdam Forcing, Early Nantes and Early Horn are all recommended for frame, cloche and early outdoor sowings. Amsterdam Forcing is probably the earliest but Early Nantes is, I find, the most reliable because it stands well through the early spring. They can be pulled finger-long or allowed to grow to intermediate size. Autumn King and St Valéry are by far the most treasured carrot sowings. Autumn King must be the best carrot for storing or standing through the winter and St Valéry is surely one of the most attractive. Its long dark red roots are a favourite for the exhibition bench.

There are, of course, many other good carrots. If you want to grow huge carrots to show off to family and friends, try Flak (it is offered for sale in gardening magazines) or Zino from Thompson and Morgan, who claim the world record with a carrot of 7lb 11½oz (approximately 3.5kg). For growing quick crops, the round-shouldered carrots, the squat fat globes, are recommended. Try Rondo or Kundulous which seem to be more resistant to splitting than many other carrots.

Cauliflowers

One of the old favourites, All the Year Round, is still going strong and still living up to its name. It is most reliable for sowing through the season and is one of the best value-for-money purchases. One packet can produce enough seeds for sowing throughout the year. Snow Prince is a good early cauliflower from spring sowings and has given me the best results in recent years, and Snowball is a reliable cauliflower, which can be sown in autumn for over-wintering in the frame or sown in a heated greenhouse in January or February.

Another favourite for me is Flora Blanca, which is excellent for exhibition and the table. So too is Barrier Reef, an Australian-bred variety, which will produce solid curds in late October when there is often a lull in harvesting in the allotment.

French beans

Some great strides have been made in producing new varieties in the past decade or so. Two of the best in my view are The Prince and Masterpiece.

Lettuce

Fortune, Suzan and All the Year Round are three of the best early lettuce which can be sown in January for early crops. Tom Thumb, a brave little lettuce, is recommended for early cloche or cold frame work. Mid-summer lettuce are always led by the succulent Webb's Wonderful; the crisp hearts are slow to bolt and with care they can be grown successionally through the summer. For those who prefer Cos lettuce, Little Gem is the quickest to mature and the most reliable of its group.

For the greenhouse, sow Kwiek which matures in November and December, and Dandie which produces, according to successional sowing between August and November, lettuce hearts between November and April. The autumn-sowing lettuce has one real champion, Valdor, although Artic King is extremely hardy.

Onions

There are many good onions — Ailsa Craig, Bedfordshire Champion, Sturon, Rijnsburger — which produce excellent harvests. These can be sown between March and April, although Ailsa Craig can be sown in January under glass for large exhibition onions. I have enjoyed growing the Kelsae and

Robinson's Mammoth onions for the very large bulbs which so fascinate visitors to gardening shows these days.

White Lisbon is a quick-growing spring onion for salads, and Paris Silverskin is recommended for pickling. Perhaps most interesting of all onions is the Japanese range, especially bred to bring ripened bulbs for use in June and July from a sowing in the previous August. The best I have grown have been Express Yellow or Senshy Semi-Globe.

Peas

There are many famous, succulent, sweet-tasting and high-yielding peas on the market and it is as well, if three or four rows are to be sown, to experiment with the varieties available. The early varieties — Little Marvel, which is excellent for cloche work, Feltham First, which lives up to its name, and Meteor and Kelvedon Wonder, which are known for their reliability — are all worth a try. One of the highest-yielding peas for later in the season is Hurst Green Shaft which is quick growing, and its resistance to downy mildew is an added bonus. Then there are two of the great peas, Show Perfection and Achievement, both recommended for the show bench, the table and the freezer.

Runner beans

This is the best 'feeder' crop on the plot. If cultivated properly, many pounds of beans can be produced for the kitchen in late summer and for the freezer for winter. Again the varieties are many and varied, with my favourites being Enorma, Prizewinner, Achievement and, of course, Scarlet Emperor. However, I have found the tastiest of all to be an old Midland strain, the Churchfield Black, which if picked young is a most tender and tasty bean.

Tomatoes

If I could grow only one variety of tomato it would be Alicante which, apart from possessing an outstanding taste, crops well in the greenhouse or out on the plot. For a heated greenhouse, Eurocross does well, and for those who like big, fleshy fruits there is Big Boy. A newcomer is Shirley from Suttons, which is an early maturing variety; it is disease resistant and has produced excellent results in my greenhouse.

For outdoor use there is the previously mentioned Alicante, with Sigmabush for medium-sized fruit from a bush variety. For those who like continental fruits, there is our favourite, Marmande, a superb-tasting tomato which is big and almost ugly, and Roma, the brightly coloured long fruits pictured on most tins of tomatoes. Roma fruits are as beautiful as Marmande are unattractive.

Varieties of less commonly grown vegetables

Recent advances by seedsmen mean that many crops that were virtually impossible to grow in a normal British summer can now be grown quite successfully. This includes crops like sweetcorn, which can be grown to its full juicy maturity, and melons which can be harvested from cold frames. There are, in addition, many other crops which can be grown to bring more variety to the family diet, and many people have found new favourites which have made the growing programme a more interesting and meals more appetising. Try some of these vegetables for a change.

Asparagus pea

Although not a true pea, it does produce tasty sweet 'winged' pods. It is sown out of doors in April and the pods are cooked whole when they are no longer than 5cm (2in) long.

Aubergines

The egg plant has to be started in a warm greenhouse in January or February and then grown on under glass. However, if you can spare a corner of the greenhouse, they are a delicious crop, especially when sliced and fried slowly.

Chinese cabbage

This is a late-growing vegetable which produces crisp and

crunchy white hearts to eat like lettuce or to cook as a cabbage. It is sown late in the season (June or July) and grown as a lettuce.

Endive
A crisp continental-style salad crop, it should be blanched by excluding light from it, either by covering with a pot or by bunching all the outer leaves and tying them up.

Florence fennel
This went out of fashion some years ago because of its annoying tendency to run to seed, but those who like to produce its sweet aniseed taste should sow early (by the end of April) so that the vegetable has a chance to reach early maturity.

Garlic
This tasty ingredient for many meals is easy to grow. Plant the cloves in February or March, leave the tip at soil level and keep weed free.

Horseradish
One of the most tasty of roots, it is used to make sauce for roast beef and fish dishes. Plant 30cm (1ft) long thongs in vertical holes in good rich soil and it will grow and grow. The roots will take over the garden if it is not kept strictly under control.

Jerusalem artichokes
This is a trouble-free crop which is very tasty when used chopped up in a winter salad or roasted like potatoes around the joint of meat. The tubers are planted in March just as potatoes are placed in trenches. Hoe around the tops occasionally through the summer until they are dug up in autumn.

Kohl rabi
The flavour of Kohl rabi is midway between a cabbage and a turnip. The edible portion is the swollen stem just above the soil level. It is sown in April or May and should be lifted when just

larger than a tennis ball. If it is allowed to grow too large it will lose its flavour.

Pumpkins
These are often grown just for fun with many people having competitions to see who can grow the heaviest. However, they can be used in the kitchen, and a colleague of mine often brings slices of pumpkin pie to work.

Salsify
This is an appetising and nutritious vegetable with a root just like a parsnip. It is eaten boiled, baked or roasted around a joint of meat. It is very hardy and can remain in the ground all winter for spring use.

Scorzonera
This is similar in appearance to salsify but has black-skinned roots and is boiled for use. Sow in April and thin out to 30cm (1ft) apart.

Sugar pea
This is another pea that can be cooked whole as the pods are completely stringless. The combination of juicy pods and sugar-sweet peas makes them an easy-to-grow delicacy.

Other crops

Recommendations for growing other vegetables are made, where appropriate, in the week-by-week summary of work on the allotment given in chapter 7.

2 Feeding the soil

The basics of gardening on an allotment plot are the same as for any other form of horticultural activity — the soil must be brought into peak condition before successful flowering, fruiting or harvesting can be achieved. To grow any plant — whether vegetables, flowers, shrubs or trees — the soil must be given all the necessary ingredients for the plant to take up to produce growth and ultimately food, fruit or flowers. Just as a piece of dough will not rise without yeast, a plant without a properly balanced diet will simply not grow to full maturity.

One of the major steps forward in gardening for me came when I started to understand the basic structure of the soil, its needs and its idiosyncracies. I well remember my grandfather explaining in detail to me that the soil was just like a mother, giving to the plant all its basic needs, just as any parent aims to provide the best for its child. Of course, the doting mother must have all the ingredients to hand if she is to provide for all the wants of her child. And so it is with the soil. Give the soil the feedstuffs in its structure and it will, with the help of water, give the plants all they require to grow to maturity.

The analogy with a young growing child continues when one talks of a balanced diet because, just like a small infant, a plant will greedily take all that it is offered. So it is important that feed is not given indiscriminately, since too much nitrogen, potash or phosphates can bring about what in the plant world is a fat, sluggish and sleepy baby, a plant too lush to bother to grow to its full potential or produce any worth-while fruit. Lushness is a condition that all gardeners must strive to avoid. It may look good; the high green sheen in the summer sunshine is an attractive sight, but without the balanced feed which brings potash into its diet, the plant will not produce a worth-while meal for the table.

Anyone who has worked with the soil knows it as a fascinating, complex mixture of many constituents, a combination which can vary considerably in its structure from county to county and even, in some urban areas where the land has been built up, from street to street. Gardeners who have worked with clay soil will know how difficult a medium it is. It is a cold, waterlogged soil which needs large quantities of farmyard manure dug into it, along with all the homemade compost that can be found to help break it down. A sprinkling of lime on the surface in the winter will help too, as it combines with the frost to break down the heavy clods.

Sandy soils are, of course, much easier to dig but they require just as much work and as much manure, compost and any other form of humus that the gardener can lay his fork on. The application of every available fork-full of humus-forming material will help sandy, quick-draining soil to become more substantial so that it can retain more easily the feeds the gardener gives it during the season. Until it has been essentially improved, sandy soil will need frequent feeding, particularly of nitrogen which is quickly lost as rainwater passes so easily through the soil. The lighter soils also need liming more often.

A great deal of manure is required for chalky soils too, but as they are naturally alkaline they do not require liming.

All the manuring and composting work should be carried out in the autumn and winter, the material being trenched or dug-in under the soil as early as possible. It is essential, though, that this is only done when the weather is fair as work on the plot when the soil is wet and tacky is highly detrimental to the soil structure which you are striving to improve. Work the soil with a fork and soon the micro-organisms will get down to the job of decomposition, breaking the earth down into a crumbly material that plants love to spread their roots into.

Making compost

The gardener needs all the humus he can lay his hands on and,

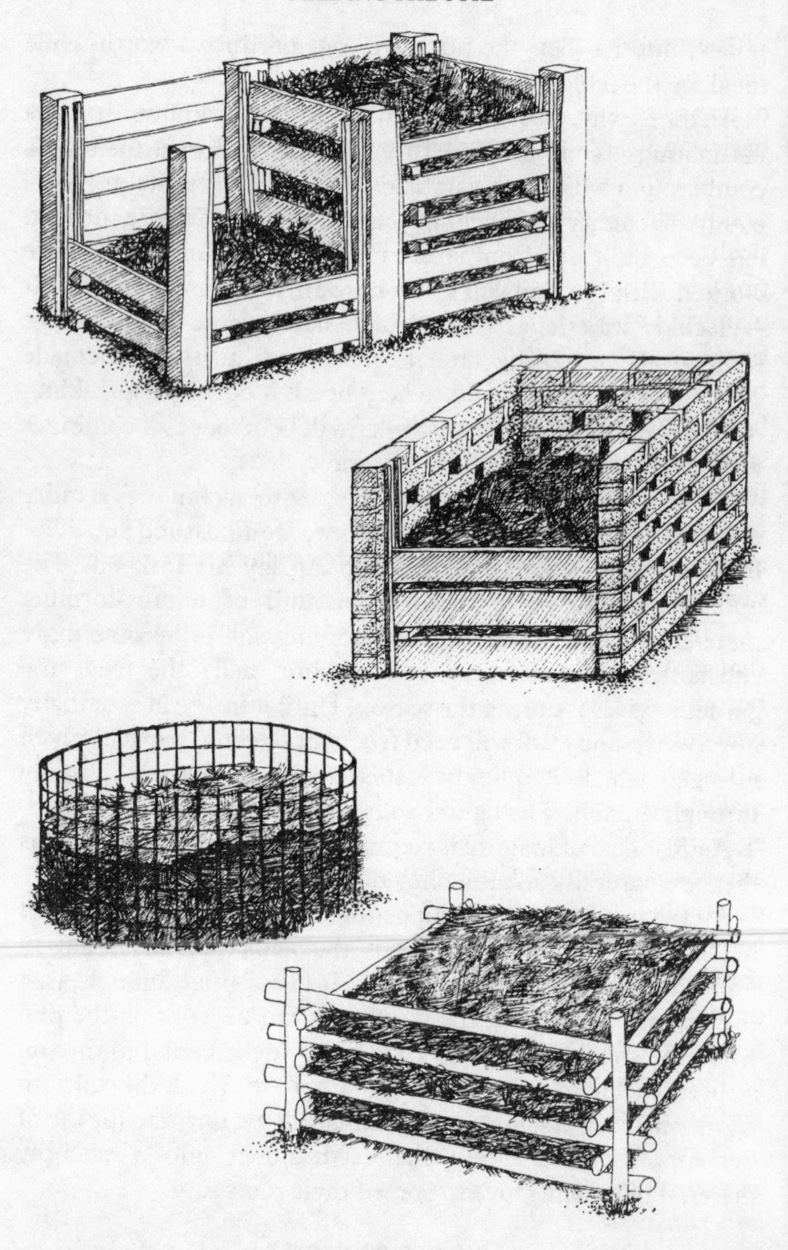

Compost heaps — wooden-framed, brick built, a circle of wire and wooden stakes

as the price of manure from farmyards and stables increases every year, especially to urban dwellers who have to pay heavily to transport the 'black gold', more gardeners are going back to basics and running a compost heap again. This provides, at no cost at all, a cheap humus that puts new heart into the plot.

Kitchen waste — cabbage stalks and leaves, pea pods, potato peelings, tea leaves, coffee grounds — can be composted to provide material suitable for digging into the ground or for using as a mulch. The waste can be collected at home in plastic bags and transported to the allotment at weekends. Then it can be mixed in with garden refuse in a frame made by knocking the bottom out of a wooden box and boring holes in the sides, by staking up a circle of wire netting or by knocking bits of wood together. There are, of course, manufactured bins, but I always feel they look out of place on an allotment. They are more appropriate to the back garden, where the need to be a little neater can make them an attractive purchase.

Whatever the method of storing the waste, it is important that it should be managed properly so that the pile does not become smelly and sour. The heap needs to heat-up and ferment so that full decomposition can take place, so it is advisable to use an activator to encourage the rapid decay that makes sweet compost quickly and efficiently. These activators, eg Garotta, Bio Recycler and Comphost, are cheap enough and are based on nitrogenous compounds which quickly break down plant materials. If you do not want to buy a specialised activator, use any spare nitrogen feeds you may already have in the allotment shed. Mix the heap up a little by covering every 25 or 30cm (10 or 12in) of waste material with the activator and a few centimetres of soil. A small sprinkling of lime occasionally will help to keep the heap sweet, rather than letting it go sour and acidy.

Many people get taken over by a desire to save every last fibre of natural material and rip up old woolly jumpers, newspapers and cardboard boxes to throw on the heap. It is important, though, not to be carried away and to remember that certain things should be discarded. Potato haulms should be burned in case they are carrying potato blight, as should brassica roots, for fear of storing up club root in the plot. Perennial weeds, such as couch grass, nettles and docks, should not be on the plot anyway, but if they are dug up, they should be burned or thrown away.

By now it is assumed that the allotment ground is on the way to becoming a viable mixture of soil and humus which can be improved year after year by generous applications of manure in the autumn. Remember that manure should ideally be well rotted and must be applied and dug into the ground at the earliest possible time. If plants are placed in soil dressed with fresh manure, their roots can easily be burned by the hotness of the decomposition process. In addition, as the process of decomposition robs the soil of nitrogen, any planting in ground laced with fresh manure can only lead to sick plants as the life-giving chemical attacks the newly arrived manure. For this reason, sprinkle a little nitro-chalk onto the plot after digging in the manure, especially if you are a little late in your manuring programme.

Nutrient sources

Now the most crucial time of the year has arrived. It is time to decide what food should be given to the soil to grow the wide range of vegetables the allotment grower will want to take home to the kitchen. How does one decide what the soil should be given? In what quantities do the various vegetables require the main feeds, nitrogen, potash and phosphates? One easy rule of thumb is to consider first just what each of the three main nutrients contribute to the growth of the plant. Table 2 will help you.

These three basic nutrients are the main ingredients which the plant requires from germination through the seedling stage to maturity when it is picked or cut by the gardener. They are available in many forms, both organic and inorganic. Table 3 analyses the various sources of nutrients and gives the percentage content of each. It is important to note, however,

Table 2 Nutrients

Nitrogen — the leaf maker

Uses	*Where found*	*When to apply*
Stimulates quick growth in plants. Improves colour and quality of leaf crops. Helps decomposition of manure, compost and other humus-making material.	In animal byproducts such as dried blood, fish blood and bone, manure, compost, fish-meal, bonemeal, nitrate of soda, nitrochalk, sulphate of ammonia.	Apply organic fertilisers such as bone-meal weeks before planting. Inorganic fertilisers should be used with extreme care.

Phosphates — the root maker

Uses	*Where found*	*When to apply*
Helps to give young plants a vigorous start. Stimulates early formation and growth. Increases germination chance for seedlings.	Although there is a great deal of phosphates in the soil structure it is mostly insoluble and usually has to be given in the form of super-phosphates.	Sprinkle super-phosphates on the ground before sowing and planting.

Potash — the flower and fruit maker

Uses	*Where found*	*When to apply*
Produces strong stiff stalks. Makes plants more vigorous and disease resistant. Improves flavour and colour of vegetables.	Wood ash, the material left after burning, is a fine potash provider but it must be bagged immediately after cooling as rain washes potash out. It is found in two main fertilisers, sulphate of potash and muriate of potash.	Wood ash can be thrown over the beds. Potash fertilisers can be used best at the end of the season to harden and ripen the vegetables.

that manure and garden compost contain very little of these essential nutrients. They are primarily used to provide humus to hold the feeds once they have been applied.

The quantity of fertiliser applied to the different sections of the garden is of paramount importance. As you will see from table 3, there are large differences in the percentage nutrient content of the various sources, so that extreme care must be shown when using substances such as sulphate of ammonia,

Table 3 Analysis of nutrient sources

Nitrogen

Organic Sources	%	*Inorganic Sources*	%
Hoof and horn	13.0	Sulphate of ammonia	21.0
Dried blood	13.0	Nitro-chalk	21.0
Fishmeal	9.5	Nitrate of soda	16.0
Bonemeal	3.2	Nitrate of potash	13.0
Garden compost	0.8	Growmore	7.0
Manure	0.7		

Phosphates

Organic Sources	%	*Inorganic Sources*	%
Bonemeal	29.0	Triple superphosphates	42.0
Boneflour	28.0	Superphosphates	20.0
Fishmeal	10.0	Growmore	7.0
Hoof and horn	2.0		
Manure	0.3		
Garden compost	0.2		

Potash

Organic Sources	%	*Inorganic Sources*	%
Mushroom compost	0.6	Sulphate of potash	48.0
Garden compost	0.4	Muriate of potash	44.0
Manure	0.5	Growmore	7.0

superphosphates or sulphate of potash. It is easy to overfeed and end up with disastrous results.

Over the years, I have seen the tragic results of overfeeding. Too much nitrogen can make a plant lush, soft and flabby; extra phosphates can burn plants, and strong applications of potash can simply stop the growth of a plant completely. Potash is available in very few things, apart from wood ash. The barrow loads of manure that have so diligently been fed into the plot are virtually devoid of potash. The use of Growmore can help because that has a 7–7–7 percentage make-up of nitrogen, phosphates and potash. However, as plants reach maturity, it is wise to use high-potash feeds such as Phostrogen or Maxicrop which can both be used for root or foliar feeding programmes, are reasonably inexpensive and easy to apply.

There are few arguments about the methods of fertilising the ground during the dormant period, but when it comes to feeding the plot during the growing season the arguments abound. Some gardeners use only organic feeds, such as bonemeal and fish, blood and bone mixture, whilst other growers prefer the inorganic fertilisers, such as nitro-chalk or nitrate of soda. As gardening correspondent for a newspaper, it has been my pleasure to talk about the growing of high-quality vegetables with some of the country's top growers, and the huge differences in their advice has never ceased to amaze me. One of them may love the quick-acting qualities of high-nitrogen nitrate of soda, whilst another with almost identical results on the show bench will not even have it in his allotment shed, let alone around the roots of his vegetables.

It is certainly true that the use of the straight fertilisers, which have grown in popularity in the past decade or so, have to be used as part of a balanced diet, a strict and meagre feeding programme where the grower knows exactly the amounts he is giving to each individual plant. These 'straights' are so quick to react and so high in their specific nutrient that untold damage can occur by over-use. Some cultivators throw the white crystals of nitrate of soda over their gardens as if they are feeding chickens with corn from a bucket. The result is often a crop, perhaps the much-admired large onions, that is so greedy to take in all the available nitrogen that it simply blows up and bursts. The similar over-use of potash fertiliser can not merely stop but kill a nicely grown plant so near to reaching its maturity.

Nitrate of soda is perhaps the most dangerous of the 'straights' because it is soluble in water and is taken up by the plant almost immediately. Its high nitrogen content attacks the humus of the carefully cultivated land and destroys the balance of the soil structure. I use it only to give spring cabbages a little boost after they have come through the winter when the nutrients have been leached from the soil. I prefer otherwise to use its sister feed, nitro-chalk, and then only very sparingly. I use it on the onion bed for the big seed onions once a month or so in the early stages, and on summer cabbages that have been 'roughed-up' a little by the spring winds and rain after planting out. Old-time gardeners I have spoken to over the past few years often recommend the use of nitro-chalk as a feed for onions and leeks as long as a matchbox of the chemical is divided absolutely equally between four plants.

For those not willing to dabble in the world of the 'straights', there are the organic base dressings such as hoof and horn and bonemeal. These can be supplemented later with one of the many liquid fertilisers on the market. These feeds can be found in any gardening shop and a look at the contents on the bottle or carton will tell you the specific contents in terms of its NPK, the nitrogen, potash and phosphate content.

Remember when using these feeds to adhere rigidly to the manufacturers' recommendations. They have not spent season after season of costly research for nothing, and the over-use of these feeds is worse than failing to use them at all. A strong feed will be taken up quickly by the roots and can destroy all the hard work done on the patch. In dry periods water the area that is to be fed before applying the fertiliser.

Soil tests

The soil and its chemical structure can be measured reasonably accurately by the use of special soil test equipment which is both simple to operate and inexpensive to purchase. The test kits come in various forms and can be used to measure the acidity of the soil and to establish the potash–nitrogen–phosphate content.

Soil acidity is measured on a pH scale from a neutral point of pH 7 where alkalinity and acidity are equal. The more alkaline, that is the more limey, the soil the higher the pH measurement; the more acidic the soil, the lower the figure. The acidity of the soil can be ascertained by a simple pH measuring instrument which is plunged into the soil. It gives the pH value of the soil as a reading on a needle scale.

Once the measurement has been established, the soil can be

treated according to its needs. If the pH level is below 6.5–7, the ground should be limed, bearing in mind that 140g per sq m (4oz per sq yd) will raise the level by about 0.5. The lime is best added in the late autumn or winter, so that it can work its way into the soil through the dormant part of the season. Do not under any circumstances lime and manure at the same time. Lime about two months after manuring and, conversely, do not apply manure or fertiliser until at least a month after liming. The combination of lime and fresh manure sets off a chemical reaction and builds up poisonous gases in the soil which can easily lead to the souring of the whole soil structure.

The pH reading can be lowered less easily but the digging in of large quantities of peat, which can be quite expensive, or a dressing of flowers of sulphur, about 70g per sq m (2oz per sq yd) will reduce the acidity.

Trace elements

The trace elements, sometimes known as the minor soil elements, are nutrients in the soil which are vital to the proper growth of food crops, although they are only required in very small quantities. These include sulphur, calcium, magnesium manganese, copper, molybdenum and chlorine. The shortage of one or more of these vital elements can severely damage the plants. For instance, mottling of the green leaves on plants suggests magnesium deficiency which can be remedied by an application of magnesium sulphate, otherwise known as Epsom salts. Any remedial work, though, must be carried out with the utmost care; the dose of Epsom salts should, for instance, be no more than 28g to 8sq m (1oz to 10sq yd). That very small dosage serves to remind the gardener that too much of the trace elements in the soil is as detrimental to the plant as too little. An iron deficiency shows up when leaves go completely green and this can be remedied with a dose of sequestrene of iron. But be warned again; too much iron can greatly damage the soil structure.

Some manures, notably seaweed fertilisers and fish manure,

can contain trace elements but the correct proportions of these substances can be found in many of the foliar feeds. These are easy to use and are reasonably inexpensive.

Specific feeding

Crop rotation will have decided what is to be grown where and when. The plot will have been drawn out and now it is time, in early spring, to work out the specific needs of individual plants. Some vegetables like certain feeds; for instance, onions and leeks thrive on nitrogen during their early growing season and it is wise to plan for their needs from an early stage. Therefore, after the garden has been planned out, peg out the diferent sections — the patches for carrots, onions, leeks — and apply the necessary fertilisers.

Brassicas
The bed that will provide cabbages, cauliflowers, kale, broccoli and sprouts should first be tested for lime. If the soil is alkaline and needs sweetening, it is essential to give the bed a liberal dressing of lime. The lime application will also cut the risk of the bed being hit by club root, the debilitating soil-borne disease that can dramatically reduce the harvest from the patch. The leafy brassicas also need considerable stores of nitrogen, which they can get from applications of organic feeds such as hoof and horn or dried blood or from the inorganic nitro-chalk or nitrate of soda.

Carrots, parsnips and beetroot
This bed must not under any circumstance be given fresh manure as this will make the roots of these vegetables split and become forked which will make them almost useless for the kitchen. These root crops provide some of the high-vitamin foods for the family and, to encourage juicy and nutritious crops, give the beds a light dressing of superphosphate of lime. This will give phosphates which are essential to provide good roots. A dressing of Growmore is also advisable about a month

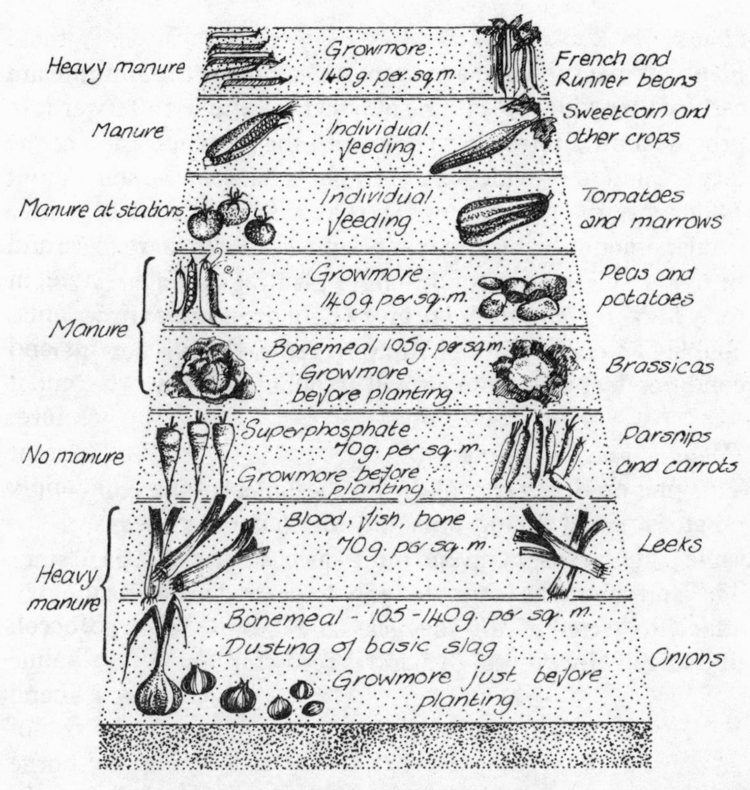

Feed the allotment to feed the plants

before sowing gets underway to provide a little more phosphate and enough nitrogen and potash to bring the bed to a good all-round growing condition.

Leeks

Growers of leeks, whether they are growing exhibition pot leeks, blanched leeks or the ordinary culinary leek, will know only too well the value of manure and well-rotted compost to this crop. This should be dug in during the autumn and given a dressing of bonemeal at 140g per sq m (4oz per sq yd). In March the leek bed can be given more nitrogen in the form of fish, blood and bone which will help to get the young leeks off to a good start.

Onions

Plenty of manure will have been dug in during the autumn and early winter with a sprinkling of bonemeal applied afterwards to provide a little nitrogen to help with the decomposition of the manure and to provide long term phosphates in the soil. About 140g per sq m (4oz per sq yd) is the recommended dose, with a similar amount being applied in January or February to start to bring the soil to peak condition for planting out in late April or early May. It is also useful to give a light dressing of Growmore a couple of weeks before planting to get the bed in near-perfect condition by bringing in a small amount of potash.

Potatoes, peas and beans

This plot produces part of the loveliest meal of the year — new potatoes, sweet young peas and luscious broad beans on the same plate as roast lamb and mint sauce, so it needs a good start. The land should be manured for potatoes and manure should be added to trenches for the peas and beans. With a general dressing of Growmore, the land is ready for use.

3 Gardening aids

There is a popular misconception that cultivation cannot be undertaken unless the gardener has a plethora of tools, a shed full of all the latest and most sophisticated equipment. In reality, all a gardener needs to get down to allotment work is a spade, a fork, a rake, a hoe, two pieces of stick and a length of string. The spade and fork are needed to dig the land, the rake to smooth down the surface for seed sowing and the hoe for keeping the weeds back and the land open to the elements. The two sticks and the string make up one of man's most important tools — the measuring line.

Other gardening tools can help considerably with the growing of food but these do not include such specialised tools as the potato hoe, onion hoe or the other ingenious and sometimes quite useless implements which have come onto the market in the past decade or two. Such gardening aids, however, as garden frames, cloches and hot beds will greatly assist the allotment man or woman to produce early seedlings which in turn accelerates the production of food to the kitchen.

Almost all of these aids can be made from wood which is often surplus to the needs of local firms — perhaps old wooden pallets, machine boxes or old window frames. Modernisation work on houses usually gives rise to large amounts of old window frames and doors. If the wood is not available in this way, the material will have to be purchased, usually quite cheaply, from wood firms who reclaim and re-sell used wood. Then, only a hammer, nails and, in some cases, pieces of glass or polythene are required.

Cloches

Cloches can extend the season at both ends, bringing forward the planting times in the early spring and protecting late crops in autumn and early winter. The season can be stretched like elastic, allowing the gardener to sow early lettuce, carrots and parsnips out in the open under the protection of the homemade cloche. The cloche is without a doubt the greatest gardening aid after the greenhouse, and can be used after the carrots and parsnips have been uncovered to bring on the earliest row of dwarf beans and to allow early sowings of runner beans and other tender plants.

After being stored for the summer, cloches come into their own later in the year for covering autumn-hearting lettuce, late summer-sown carrots and for October sowings of spinach. In November, another year of beans and peas can be started by sowing these two staple crops under the protection of polythene. Otherwise the sowings of these vegetables, even if the correct varieties are used, can be a gamble out in the open.

One of the great advantages of cloches to the allotment grower is the fact that they can be made for next to nothing. Some of my gardening friends simply use a long narrow sheet of polythene across the width of the garden, weighted down at both ends and at the sides, to warm the soil before sowing seeds that are difficult to germinate in early spring, like carrots and parsnips.

Polythene sheeting

This is the most simple of gardening aids, but it warms up the soil and leaves it dry and crumbly, an ideal environment for sowing seeds. However, it does tend to attract slugs, anxious to get into warmer areas, so use with care, although one gardener I know puts down sheeting to attract the slugs and then goes around picking them off to clear the ground before planting.

Polythene sheeting can be useful as it is, but with a little extra work it is easy to construct a perfectly adequate cloche. Simply nail polythene strips down over a wooden frame, as shown, and

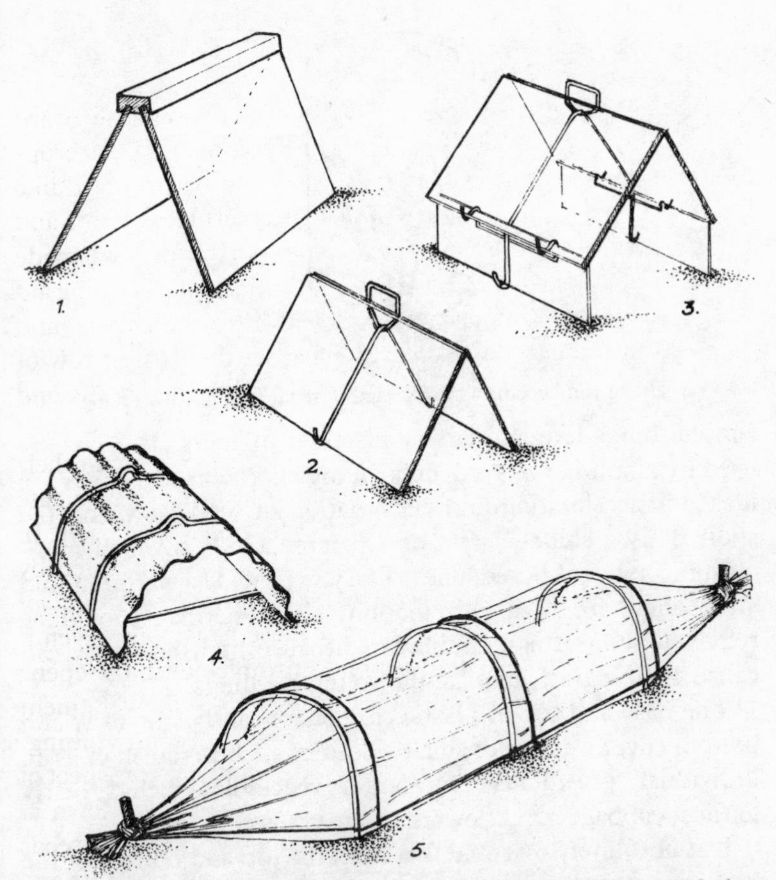

Cloches come in all shapes and sizes: 1 wooden-groove; 2 glass tent; 3 glass barn; 4 proprietary plastic cloche, and 5 polythene tunnel

then fix the framework to the soil with a camping peg or similar implement. These are light and easy to move about and place in position, as are all the polythene-covered cloches illustrated.

Another useful polythene cover is the tunnel. A length of polythene is held into place by galvanised steel semi-hoops; one side can be lifted for ventilation and for watering which is an added advantage. These are usually priced quite competitively, especially when compared to glass and plastic cloches.

Simple covers

Small individual covers can be made for single plants by using

A jam jar can become a mini-greenhouse for individual seedlings

simple things like jam jars or plastic containers. Jam jars are used by a number of gardeners on my allotment site. They are ideal for accelerating and germination of seeds sown on the spot. This includes carrot and parsnip seeds sown in mini-clusters on top of bored holes. The jars provide a warm, humid atmosphere for seed germination, although they should be removed soon after germination because high humidity can cause damping-off amongst the young seedlings.

The base and top of plastic containers can be cut away and used to cover a group of small seedlings such as radish or as an individual 'greenhouse' for larger vegetables such as early lettuce, cabbage, cauliflowers and marrows.

It is absolutely essential that both the top and bottom of the plastic container are removed to allow ventilation. The top can either be cut off, or unscrewed. If this is not done there will be a build-up of humidity in the enclosed area with the plant transpiring a considerable amount of liquid which can lead to the damping-off of the plant.

Glass cloches

These are the most rigid of all cloches which can stand up to the winter winds much better than polythene or plastic. The simplest glass cloche is made by clipping two pieces of glass together, and several firms make easy-to-use clips to hold them firmly in place. Otherwise, grooves can be cut into strips of wood and the glass pushed into place.

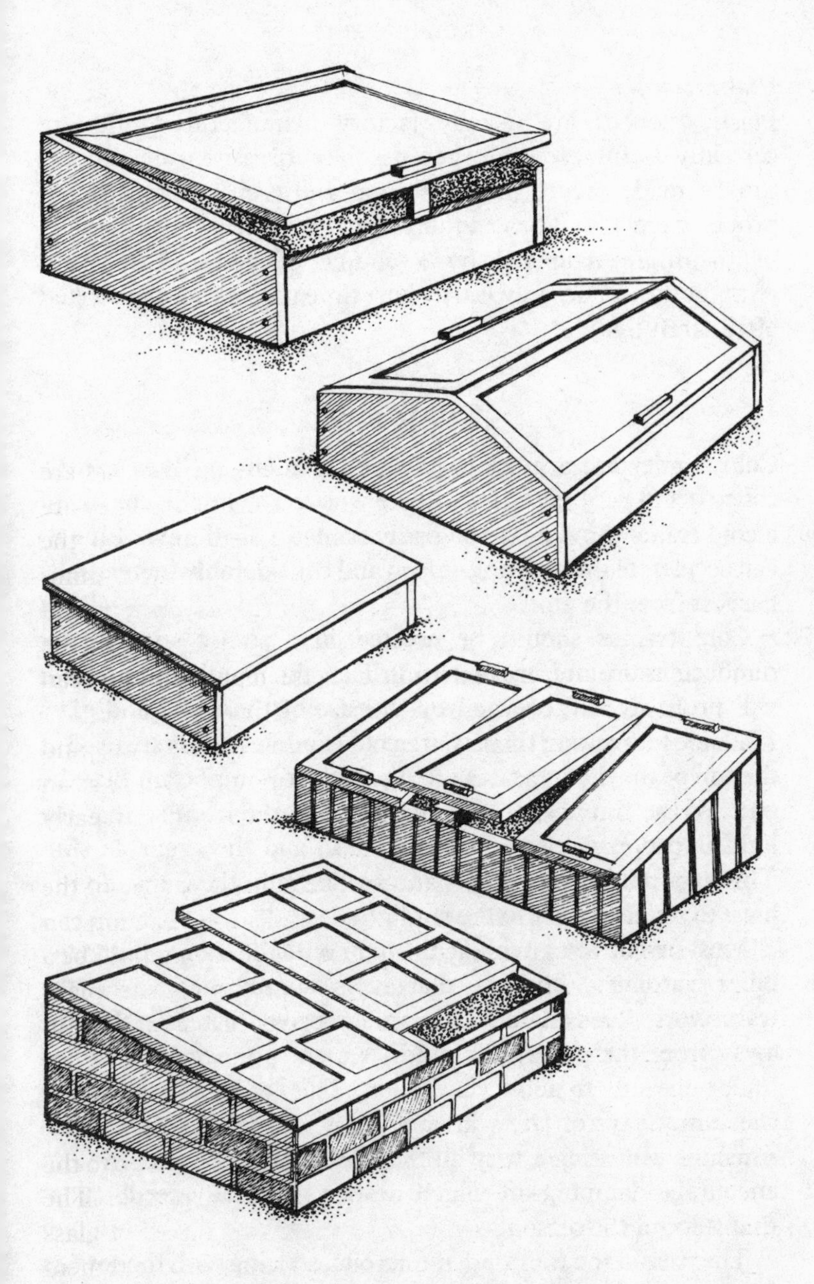

More types of cloche; a box with a sheet of glass on top can be just as effective as the more sophisticated designs

Plastic cloches

Plastic cloches are usually factory manufactured and are certainly useful, especially because they are easy to move about, can be made secure in the ground and are draught-proof if properly erected. They can, however, be expensive, and many of them are damaged by a couple of years in sub-zero temperatures, and only last a short time unless they are looked after carefully.

Cold frames

Cold frames are a must in anyone's garden and they can be constructed very easily from spare wood. The intelligent use of a cold frame (how it was so badly named I shall never know!) can accelerate the growing season and considerably increase the harvest from the plot.

Cold frames should be erected in a sunny spot. Their dimensions are not important; in fact, the length and breadth will probably be governed by the size of the wood and glass available for making them. Often old window frames are used as the top of the 'light' as it is often called. It is important that the back of the frame should be higher than the front so that the light is propped forward facing south and the available sun. This ensures that the plants and seedlings in the frame do not have to stretch to get to the sunlight.

Most people tend to hinge the light onto the frame, but many older gardeners suggest that it is simply held over the framework. This enables the frame to be ventilated on the side away from the prevailing wind. A plant pot can be propped under one side to allow ventilation. This, of course, is vital in the sunny days of late winter or early spring when the warm sunshine can bring a very humid atmosphere to the frame and encourage damping-off which destroys so many seedlings at that stage of the season.

The uses of the frame are numerous, starting with the sowing of broad beans and peas in November to over-winter in the frame for planting out at the end of March. The frame need never be idle; if it is not filled with boxes or pots of cauliflowers, dwarf and runner beans, lettuce or cabbage, it can be used as a mini-bed for the earliest carrots, radish, mustard and cress. Later in the year it can be used for cucumbers, melons or squashes.

Whenever the frame is in use it is vital that it is ventilated properly. In winter the merest crack of air is enough; allow great gaps in the frame and the frost can quickly get in and damage the plants and seedlings beyond recovery. Unnecessary watering must also be avoided for an atmosphere which is too moist can easily lead to trouble. In spring, air can be allowed in by propping up the frame light with a small pot or a wedge of wood. To retain the day's sun, however, it is advisable — and this is not always possible for the average allotment grower — for the frame light to be closed early in the afternoon or early evening to retain some of the heat.

The glass must always be kept clean inside and out, and any cracks or holes must be stopped up with putty to prevent rain or cold winds getting into the frame. At the first suspicion of frost, dry sacking or similar material should be placed over the frame light, making sure that the gap between the side and top of the frame is covered completely. The sacking can be held in place with carefully placed pieces of wood or bricks.

Hot beds

More and more people are now returning to one of the older methods of achieving sufficient heat to germinate seeds — the use of a warm frame or 'hot bed'. A cold frame can easily be converted to a hot bed by placing the whole frame on a bed of manure, leaf mould and compost. This is the traditional way, but a friend of mine grows more than 11,000 plants in a row of hot beds in his back garden on top of rotting lawn cuttings. It works for him — he wins the West Midlands Municipal Gardener of the Year Competition every year!

The warmth given out by the decomposing manure and other organic substances converts the cold frame into a mini-

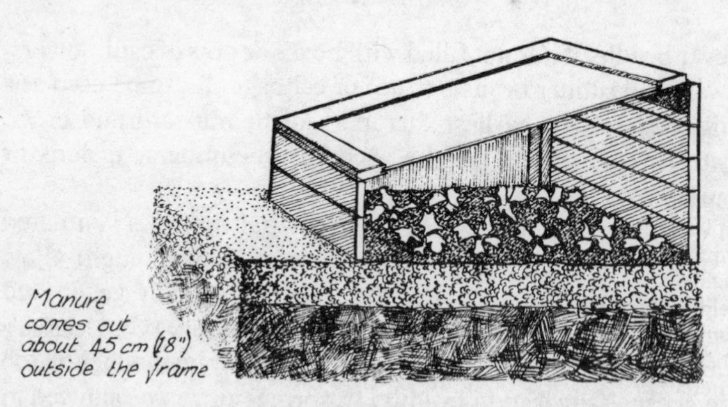

A hot bed can provide a steady stream of seedlings. Dig in manure or lawn cuttings just below the soil surface

greenhouse; virtually every plant can be started in this way. The leaf mould is mixed with the manure as a moderation agent to give a steady long-lasting heat rather than the harsh heat manure alone would give. An ideal hot bed would be built onto a mixture of manure and leaf mould with the area of manure mixture exceeding the area of the frame by at least 45cm (18in) in each direction.

A little patience is needed after the construction of the hot bed because the first heat from the ground is rather hot and steamy. Leave the frame light open for the steam to escape and after six or seven days place a layer of soil, perhaps 25cm (9in) deep at the front rising up parallel to the glass. Wait again for a day or two for the soil to warm up and then the seed can be sown in boxes or pots.

In a really serious hot bed the boxes or pots should be sunk to the rim in the soil and it is advisable to have a thermometer handy to keep a close watch on the soil temperature. If it creeps above 21°C (70°F), improve the ventilation. As well as using the hot bed for germinating seeds for transplanting later, try growing some very early carrots to pull when finger-long. Use Early Nantes or Amsterdam Forcing. Radish and lettuce can be started in the same way.

The frame will maintain useful heat for about three months; when the frame is emptied of its seedlings and young plants it can be used for growing cucumbers, melons or early courgettes. The decomposed manure will provide the ideal growing medium for these plants and the frame will give them the protection they need if they are to reach maturity early in the year.

Electric propagators

Heated propagators are becoming one of the great tools of gardeners anxious to steal a step on nature and get their seeds off to a very early start. I have used electrically heated propagators for a number of years now to germinate onions, leeks, early cauliflowers, cucumbers and scores of different varieties of flowers. They help to cut the enormous cost of producing early seedlings as the expense of using a propagator, however large, is a very small fraction of the price of heating a greenhouse simply for germinating seeds. In the past I have cut the greenhouse in half, with the use of polythene sheets, in a bid to cut the cost of late December and early January heating, but even that is a relatively expensive business when only a few pans or trays of seeds are being started.

So, soon after Christmas every year, the propagator is retrieved from the loft, dusted down and put into action to start the onions and leeks. The operations so efficient and rapid that special care must be taken that the emerging seedlings are not left unattended for too long, otherwise they will pass the 'crook' stage. That is how fast things can germinate and grow in the propagator.

The utmost care is required with watering in these propagators. It is easy to overwater and to create a 'steamy' atmosphere which can lead to damping-off or botrytis. It is only necessary to water the trays from the bottom when the seeds are sown. They will need no further moisture until they are moved out of their 'hot-tray' home.

It is essential to guard against strong January sunshine which can often catch the early gardener napping. Although the sophisticated machines keep the heat of the propagators in the region of 20°C (85°F), the new year sun can easily 'sizzle' the tender seedlings if they are left in a sun-baked greenhouse. It is therefore vital to ensure that the propagators are shaded on sunny days, and the adjustable ventilator in the plastic lid should be kept open to give adequate ventilation to the germination area.

My propagator, which cost me something in the region of £20, has repaid me many times over and with careful use it can lengthen the all-too-short growing season for gardeners of all interests. Although there can be problems with heat and ventilation, careful watering, shading and a weekly spraying of Cheshunt Compound will keep the dreaded damping-off disease at bay.

Watering equipment

The simple hose pipe and watering can are two of the most important gardening aids. Although the nutrients are important to a plant's growth to maturity, it is water that is most vitally needed. Feed can be thrown at the plants, gram upon gram, but unless the soil is moist the plant cannot take it up. As one old gardener told me: 'The plant needs water to take the food because I have yet to see a plant with a knife and fork.'

The watering process for the gardener should start, if the ground is dry, before the seed is sown or the plants set out in the ground. Plants started off with a moist root-run have everything in their favour and so I run the watering can along the carrot or beetroot row before sowing. This will set up a moisture store for the germinating seed and do away with the necessity of watering over the top of the new seed drill which may wash away the seed.

Water the trowel holes where plants, especially moisture-loving brassicas, are to be transplanted. It is essential, too, to water plants in pots or boxes before they are transplanted.

Transplanting leafy plants in late spring or early summer can sometimes prove difficult during warm spells. Many plants can droop quite dramatically; if this happens I like to put a pinch of Phostrogen or a drop of foliar feed in the water and then place sheets of newspaper over each plant. This will prevent a rapid loss of moisture through the leaves, and after a couple of days the plants will stand up straight and true again.

Watering can

The watering can must be the simplest of all the gardening equipment in the garden shed, yet it is possible to use it to the detriment of plants. The soil around a plant can be violently disturbed when water is gushed around its roots from a simple spout, sometimes leaving the root system open to the drying sun. On the other hand, the use of a rose on the end of the spout can often prevent the plant getting sufficient water down to its thirsty roots. A rose should really be used only on young seedlings recently planted out and on seed drills.

The ideal way of watering was used by my grandfather who, I remember, used to wrap a piece of sacking around the spout neck so that the flow from the can was restricted to just a dribble. It takes a little longer but it gets the job done better. It pays to take your time when watering and ensure that the plants get enough moisture. It is far better that only half the plants get a watering on any given day, rather than all the plants getting 50 per cent or less of their basic requirements. If only small amounts of water are given to the plants, their roots will turn towards the surface to chase the water in the top soil. If the roots are lying near the surface of the ground they will be susceptible to further drying out in the warm periods. Ultimately, the plants get weaker rather than stronger.

Hose pipes

The same rule applies to hose pipes; they must be used properly so that the roots of the plants get a soaking rather than the ground getting a light sprinkling. If a sprinkler system is used, it must be in place over one particular patch of the allotment for at least twenty to thirty minutes in summer.

If these simple rules of watering are not followed, all the hard work of digging the plot to provide inducement for the roots to go well down into the soil is lost. To attract the roots to the top by drops of water on the surface, however often it is done, is to waste precious water, time, labour and the plant's potential.

4 Growing all year round

Anyone hoping to make the best use of an allotment must ensure that he or she can produce staple crops like brassicas, lettuce and carrots for as many weeks of the year as possible. In the case of brassicas — the leafy family of cabbage, cauliflowers, sprouts and broccoli — it is possible, with a little care and simple planning, to have greens with the meat and potatoes every Sunday of the year. With lettuce, the weather admittedly can play quite a large part in the success rate, but it should still be possible to have young, tender lettuce hearts for the table for most of the year. It is also possible to have carrots always to hand, pulling them early from frames or cloches in the spring, through the summer months from spring sowings and on into the autumn and winter under cloches or with the shoulders of the maincrops being covered with soil in the plot.

These are just three of the main vegetables that can be made available to the keen plot holder throughout the year. There are others. Leeks can be grown for late summer and autumn from one early sowing and the later sowings can stand through the winter. Spinach and parsnips are also good winter feedstuffs. However, when it comes to making the most of brassicas, carrots and lettuce, there is much planning to be done, and it is most important to select the correct varieties for the particular time of year.

Cabbages

To grow cabbages successfully throughout the year it is necessary to divide the sowing programme into early summer maturing cabbage, summer maturing cabbage, winter and savoys and spring cabbage.

Early summer maturing cabbage should be sown in January or early February, the plants being transplanted in March, if the weather is kind, or April. These sowings in heat will provide the earliest cabbages in June and take over from the spring cabbage.

Summer maturing cabbage is a crucial cabbage if the whole programme is to be continued throughout the year. It should be sown in late March or early April, transplanted in May and harvested in July, August and early September. Included in this section is the red cabbage which is sown in April and ready for the pickling jars in late August and September.

Winter cabbage and savoys are the brave members of the brassica family that can stand for months in the worst that winter can throw at them. These are sown in late April or early May in a seed bed on the plot.

Spring cabbage is another courageous crop and a favourite in many families, including mine, for its special taste at a quiet time in the harvesting of vegetables from the plot. It is sown in late July, transplanted in late September and early October to give hearts in April. It is a very important crop, and it can become even more useful if the number of cabbages in each row is doubled. Every other plant can then be pulled prematurely to provide winter greens in January and February.

Chinese cabbage can be boiled as any other cabbage or it can have its leaf ribs cooked like asparagus or seakale. It can also be used raw for salads. It is sown directly into the cropping site in July and, as long as it is always given adequate moisture, it will produce quite large hearts for early Autumn. Table 4 provides a sowing plan which will enable you to pick cabbages every weekend of the year.

A glance down the harvesting column will show that the plan provides for cabbages from late May of one year to the same time the year after. The programme begins with the sowing of early summer maturing cabbage in January and February and continues through the spring and summer to the sowings of July and August. Only the incorrect selection of varieties will stand in the way of a hearty cabbage every Sunday. Table 5 indicates

Table 4 Cabbage – all-year-round plan

Cabbage	Sow under cloches	Plant in open	Sow out-doors	Trans-plant outdoors	Harvest
Early summer	January to February	March to April			late May to June
Summer			March to early May	June and July	August to September
Autumn			April to to May	June to late July	late August to October
Winter Savoys			late April to June	June to August	October November December January
Spring			July to August	September to October	April May June

the successional sowings required throughout the year of the different seasonal varieties.

Cauliflowers

This vegetable is one of the most challenging of all the crops on the plot because it is genuinely quite difficult to grow and because the incidence of pest damage is very high.

The cauliflower for the real enthusiast starts in late September or early October with the sowing of special varieties in a cold frame. These varieties — Dok, Snowball and All the year Round — are left in the cold frame through the winter and then transplanted out in the open ground in the spring. They are then ready for cutting in May. This gives the earliest possible cauliflower heads, beating the spring sowings which

Table 5 Cabbage – seasonal varieties

Cabbage	Sow	Plant out
Early summer Greyhound Hispi	January to February	March to April
Summer Golden Acre June Star Winnigstadt	March to April	April to May
Autumn Hispi (successional) Primo	May to early June	August to September
Winter savoys Celtic Christmas Drumhead January King Savoy King	April to May	June to July
Spring April Durham Early Harbinger Offenham Wheeler's Imperial	July to August	September to October
Red Cabbage Red Drumhead	March to April	August to September

are started in a heated greenhouse in January or February. These will head in June, with the mid-season crop following on to give cauliflowers throughout August, September and October. The autumn-heading plants are started in late May and give harvests in October and November, with the winter crops being started in the last couple of weeks of May.

Whatever time of the year cauliflowers are grown, it is particularly important to keep the plants growing steadily. In dry periods they must be watered almost daily to ensure

Table 6 Cauliflower – seasonal varieties

Cauliflower	Sow	Harvest
Earlies		
All the Year Round Alpha Polaris Snowball	January to February	early June onwards
Mid-season		
All the Year Round Dominant Snow King	April to May	August to October
Autumn		
All the Year Round Autumn Giant Barrier Reef Flora Blanca Snowball	late May	October to November
Winter		
English Winter White Queen Snow White Walcheren Winter Thanet	mid-May	March to April
Overwintering		
All the Year Round Dok Snowball	late September and October	May to June

continuous growing. Early fortnightly feeds should be high in nitrogen to produce large strong leaves to protect the curds, with potash feeds being given to bring the heads to maturity as quickly as possible. The plants should be sprayed regularly with systemic insecticide to stop aphid and caterpillar attack. Table 6 provides the sowing and harvesting times of the different varieties of cauliflower.

Carrots

To pull carrots throughout the growing season, it is essential to choose the correct varieties for each of the vital sowing dates in

Table 7 Carrots – seasonal varieties

Carrots	Sow	Harvest
First Earlies Amsterdam Forcing Early Nantes Early Scarlet Horn	Can be sown in hot bed in January/ February, then under cloches and successionally through to April.	Pull when finger-long.
Intermediates Chantenay Red James Scarlet Red Intermediate	Should be sown from early March through to late April.	Allow to grow longer for summer crops.
Maincrops Autumn King Flak Juwarot St Valéry Zino	Some of these varieties can be sown early, but for storing and over-winter sow early May.	Can grow to full maturity for storing in sand and peat or leaving in ground.

the year. Quick-growing smaller carrots are needed for early winter sowings, intermediate roots for mid-summer and maincrop carrots for late summer and autumn and for standing through the winter. Sowing and harvesting times for the different varieties of carrot are given in table 7.

The early carrot varieties are best for catch-cropping and intercropping, and Early Nantes is especially good. The tasty round-shouldered carrots like Rondo and Kundulus are also recommended for this, being particularly useful because of their ability to stand for long periods without splitting. They are both suited, because of their squat shape, for use on shallow soils and small plots.

Lettuce

The wide selection of lettuce provided by seedsmen over the past twenty years or so means that it is technically possible to have lettuce from the plot (even if it is from the cloche, frame or greenhouse) for the whole of the year. The growing of lettuce throughout the year is the ultimate challenge to the successional sowing gardener and it can only be achieved by careful planning and cultivation programmes.

Fortune and Winter Density are especially good for early sowing and others, like Webb's Wonderful and Salad Bowl, are excellent for mid-season growing. Then there are the lettuce especially bred for winter use, the quaintly named Kwiek, Kloek and Dandie. In between all of these, there are lots of other lettuce, many of them superb eaters like Suzan or Little Gem, to fill in through the various sowing times in the year. For outside growing in the winter, the bravest of all, and certainly the most successful I have tried, is Valdor. A growing programme to ensure lettuce from the plot throughout the year is given in table 8.

Table 8 Lettuce – all-year-round plan

Variety of lettuce	Jan	Feb	Mar	Apr	May	June	July	Aug	Sept	Oct	Nov	Dec
Fortune	—	—										
All the year round		—	—	—	—							
Suzan												
Trocaderao Improved				—	—	—						
Lobjots												
Little Gem	—	—	—	—	—	—	—	—	—			
Winter Density		—	—	—	—	—	—	—	—			
Salad Bowl				—	—	—						
Buttercrunch				—	—	—						
Great Lakes				—	—	—						
Sigmahead			—	—	—							
Windermere	—	—	—	—	—							
Avondefiance						—	—	—				
Arctic King		—	—	—	—	—		—	—	—		
Valdor								—	—	—		
Avon Crisp						—	—	—				
Webb's Wonderful				—	—	—						
Greenhouse:												
Dwiek								—	—			
Dandie								—	—	—		
Kloek									—	—	—	
Magiola										—	—	

Other brassicas

The other members of the brassica family — sprouting broccoli, kale and Brussel sprouts — are essential to the dedicated gardener who wishes to grow all year round. They will provide green vegetables from August, when the autumn sprouting broccoli comes into its own, through to April when the kale will still be producing curly and crispy leaves. All these plants grow quite tall and require considerable care in the autumn when they need to be anchored firmly into the ground to protect them from the winds and rains of winter. They all stand for considerable times too, so periodical feeds of a general fertiliser will produce high-quality crops. Table 9 gives sowing and harvesting times for sprouting broccoli, kale and Brussel sprouts.

Table 9 Brassicas – growing plan

Brassicas	Sow	Harvest
Sprouting broccoli		
Autumn		
Autumn Spear	April to May	August to September
Express Corona		
Green Duke (dwarf)		
Italian Sprouting		
Spring		
Early Purple Sprouting	May	March to April
Improve White Sprouting		
Nine Star Perennial		
Perennial		
Purple Sprouting		
Kale		
Pentland Brig	April to May	February to April
Tall Green Curled		
Thousandhead		
Brussel sprouts		
Bedford Fillbasket	March to April	September to February
Citadel		
Peer Gynt		
Perfect Line		
Roodnerf-Early Button		

5 Pests and diseases

Regardless of advances in science and the introduction of new insecticides and fungicides, the gardener is still forever at war in his vegetable plot. Despite the use of modern poisons and tonics, pests and diseases are still as prevalent as ever unless preventative measures are regularly taken by the grower. Man has continued to fight these pests and diseases over the centuries, first with washes of natural insect-killing liquids and then with scientifically produced insecticides and fungicides.

Disease particularly attacks plants that have the slightest tendency to be weak, insipid or sick, so the first rule in the garden is to produce strong, vigorous plants which will be resistant to disease. Another important step is to spray with the new systemic sprays before there is any sign of infestation, on the premise that prevention is better than a cure. People who would rather use only natural sprays can use nicotine mixtures, derris dust or liquid to ensure that insects do not set up home in the beans or beetroot rows.

The systemics are particularly useful as plants take up the chemical into their systems and when a blackfly or greenfly sucks the sap it gets a drop of the deadly poison at the same time. Fungicides are also taken up into the system and fight sickness and disease from inside. This method is more reliable than the contact sprays which kill only by direct hits on the aphid or other pest. In a tall, lush-growing row of beans there can be a lot of misses, especially as blackfly often cling to the undersides of leaves.

There are also many natural and old-fashioned methods of keeping pests at bay or for killing them once they have arrived. A gardening friend of mine reckons that pests like the pea weevil can be kept away from the pea row by throwing wood ash from the allotment fire over the plants. It works he says, because the pests do not like the dusty conditions, and he swears that it's successful!

Apart from the usual insect pests that abound on allotment sites, there are many others which spraying and good cultivation cannot cure. The best gardeners can follow all the strictest rules of horticulture, use all the best fertilisers and still have their harvests ruined by outside forces. These include not only thieves and vandals but a mixture of natural enemies such as mice, rabbits, foxes and birds. If these are all beaten — and that is a very tall order — there is still the wind, the weeds and two of man's close friends, the cat and dog.

Foxes

These are troublesome throughout the country now that they have infiltrated into urban areas and made allotment sites their homes and playgrounds. These cunning animals like nothing more than to roll over in a seed bed just as dawn comes up over the allotment site. They cause damage too as they chase each other, or perhaps a potential victim, over beds of carrots, onions and leeks. A small wire-netting fence around the boundary helps to keep them at bay. They can easily jump over it, but the small fence makes them suspicious enough to loll about somewhere else.

Rabbits

Rabbits are again on the increase and, since their favourite foods are carrots and lettuce, it is obvious what a problem they can be for the gardener. If they are a nuisance to your particular plot, the only way to stop them is to put up wire-netting, but it must be buried to a depth of about 30cm (1ft) to stop them burrowing their way into the plot. Again the fence would not stop a determined rabbit getting in, but it does make it that little more difficult and makes a neighbour's carrots seem that little more appetising.

Mice

These are a particular nuisance in the cold periods of spring when, in their desperate search for fresh food, they dig up and eat freshly sown pea seeds. Some people, badly hit by mice, soak their seeds in paraffin before sowing. Traps and carefully positioned poison (under sheds to protect birds and small children) are the best ways of dealing with these fast-breeding pests.

Cats and dogs

These two domestic animals can, between them, help to keep foxes, mice and rabbits away, but their short cuts across the plot can cause chaos in a seed bed and seriously disrupt the plant production line, especially if they think they can smell something interesting just below the surface. Fences help to persuade them to walk around the plot and a sprinkling of anti-cat dust around seed beds can help to deter them.

Weeds

Many gardeners are obsessed by weeds and spend much of their time trying to discover a miracle cure to eradicate those that always seem to outgrow the plants that man attempts to produce for food. Yet many weeds can be checked by simple cultivation work. For instance, all perennial weeds — couch grass, nettles and dandelions — should be forked out and burned during the digging of the plot. All the annual weeds should be dug into the ground as a green manure to help to improve the texture of the soil.

The one problem spot is the path, the area around it and the boundaries, especially if the neighbouring plot holder's garden is not as clean and free of weeds as it might be. These can be eliminated by the use of the very sophisticated systemic weedkillers which can quickly destroy whole clusters of weeds right down to their root tips.

Winds

The cold, dry winds of spring can wipe out hours, weeks and months of work. These cutting winds can often take all the life out of early seedlings, cabbage, leeks and onions being the main victims. Windbreaks of plastic or wire netting or plastic strips or polythene on a wooden frame can help to protect plants against the harsh effects of wind. If plants do become slightly blanched by the winds, apply small doses of nitro-chalk to inject nitrogen quickly into the plant's system and help them back to greenness again.

Thieves and vandals

The man who steals other people's produce is usually too lazy to accept the challenge of growing food himself and lives off the efforts of others. The vandal, the thug who damages wantonly, is an even sadder case. The senseless damage to plots perpetrated in sneak attacks under the cover of darkness is contemptible. Vandals are unfortunately unbeatable since they can break through the best security.

Table 10 lists alphabetically the main types of pest encountered on the allotment, the damage caused and the recommended method of control.

Table 10 How to recognise and treat common pests and diseases

Pest	Damage	Control
Aphids	Greenfly, blackfly and woolly aphids suck the sap from a wide range of plants, making them sick and less productive. Infestation is obvious to the eye.	Spray with nicotine mixture, derris, malathion or Cropsaver when infestation is obvious, or with Tumblebug, Rapid, Sybol 2 or other systemic insecticide fortnightly to prevent infestation.

Bean beetle	Lays eggs in the pods of broad beans. Apart from the resultant curved grubs, there is also fear of fungal or bacterial disease.	Destroy rather than compost infested plants and, if seeds are kept for the following year's sowing, check seed thoroughly. Fortnightly spraying with systemic insecticide helps to stave off infestation.
Bean weevil	Eats semicircular holes from the edges of bean and pea leaves and the important nodules on the roots.	Dust or spray with derris.
Blackfly	*see* Aphids.	
Blight	Hits tomatoes and potatoes, leaving brown blotches over leaves and stems. The disease leaves sunken areas on potato tubers.	Spray regularly, once a fortnight, with liquid copper fungicide or Bordeaux Powder.
Botrytis	A grey mould disease prevalent in greenhouses or cold frames where insufficient ventilation is available. Grey patches of fur appear on stems, leaves and even on fruit. Tomatoes are particularly susceptible.	Adequate ventilation must be provided for plants grown in greenhouses or frames. Remove leaves hit by disease as soon as possible and spray with a fungicide every ten days.
Cabbage root fly	Young plants become stunted and flag in sun as maggots burrow into the root system.	For prevention apply Root Guard, Soil Pest Killer or Bromophos in the planting hole.
Canker	Dark brown or black patches on the shoulders of parsnips lead to root becoming soft and rotten.	Lime the row before sowing as canker thrives in acid soil. Try Tender and True variety which is more resistant to canker.

Capsids	Attacks the leaves of fruit trees leaving puckered brown spots and tiny holes.	Spray every ten days with liquid malathion, ensuring that the trees and bushes get treated as well as the ground around them.
Carrot root fly	Leaves go rusty as fly maggot burrows into the root leaving nasty brown inedible areas.	No cure once the crop is infected. For prevention, sprinkle Bromophos or Root Guard along the rows whilst sowing or thinning.
Caterpillars	The biggest pest problem for brassica growers. Caterpillars leave holes in all brassicas and, if left unchecked, can devastate the whole crop.	Keep a close watch on the crop, picking off the early arrivals if possible. Otherwise spray with malathion or derris when infestation is obvious to the eye.
Celery beetle	Blue oval beetles eat the the leaves and, if left unchecked, will attack the heart.	Dust with derris dust at first sight.
Celery heart rot	Bacteria turns the heart soft, brown and mushy.	Bacteria can only get into the plant through wounds caused by careless cultivation or by slug attack. Take care and keep slugs at bay with bait or liquid slug killer.
Celery leaf spot	A fungal disease which is spread rapidly by spores bringing small brown spots to the leaves.	Softly grown celery are particularly susceptible so feed with high-potash fertiliser. Spray seedlings with benomyl, Bordeaux Mixture or a copper fungicide every fortnight.
Chocolate spot	Small dark brown spots show on leaves and dark streaks on stems. The disease produces stunted plants.	Apply a good general feed to the row before seeding and try to sow on limed ground. Lift and destroy any infected plants and spray others with Benlate fungicide every ten days.

Clubroot	First indication is the flagging of brassicas in the sun. Roots are knobbly with 'finger and toe' disease.	Brassicas should be planted on limed ground as clubroot thrives on acid soils. Ground can be cleansed with the use of Jeyes Fluid or natural cleanser Armillatox. The plants can also be dipped into calomel paste before planting.
Cutworms	Can sever plants at ground level by attacking roots and stems.	Rake in Bromophos, Soil Pest Killer or Root Guard along the rows before planting.
Damping-off	Seedlings die in seed bed or box. This is often caused by overcrowding and insufficient ventilation in frames or greenhouse.	Sow thinly and spray regularly with Cheshunt Compound. Keep frames and greenhouses well ventilated at all times.
Downy mildew	Yellow blotches appear on leaves, particularly lettuce and spinach. On onion plants leaves turn grey.	Spray infected plants with Bordeaux Mixture, Zenib or any systemic fungicide. Repeat at fortnightly intervals.
Earwigs	Holes appear in leaves or flower buds.	Spray or dust with derris or a BHC - based insect killer.
Flea beetle	A serious pest to many plants, especially turnips and swedes. Eats holes in leaves and, if left unchecked, can completely defoliate a row.	Seeds which are treated with gamma-HCH dust before sowing are less likely to be affected. Dust seedlings with derris when emerging and again at first sign of attack.
Fritfly	Maggots damage seedling plants, especially sweetcorn. The plant gets weak and sickly and flags in the sunshine.	Spray with Sybol 2 every ten days or dust around the base of the plant with derris.
Gall weevil	Grubs cause severe swellings on the stems of many plants, cabbage being particularly susceptible.	Use Soil Pest Killer or Root Guard around the base of the plant. All infected plants must be uprooted and destroyed.
Greenfly	*see* Aphids.	

Leaf miners	Maggots mine through the leaf structure and a bad infestation can ruin a whole crop. Leaves turn brown and plant becomes stunted.	Pick off all affected leaves and spray the rest with any systemic insecticide every fortnight. Feed the crop with liquid fertiliser to encourage new tops to grow.
Leaf spot	Discoloured spots on leaves and black dots on stems confirm this disease.	Spray with copper fungicide Benlate, Dithane 945 or Bordeaux Mixture at first sign of trouble and every ten days thereafter.
Leatherjackets	A larvae that damages the root systems of plants.	Dust planting holes with Bromophos or diazinion.
Leek moth	Holes tunnelled in leek leaves by moth caterpillars.	Caterpillars can be picked off if the crop is examined regularly. Otherwise spray with nicotine or malathion at fortnightly intervals.
Mealy bugs	Sap-sucking pests which can destroy greenhouse crops.	Spray with malathion or Sybol 2.
Mildew	*see* Powdery mildew.	
Millipedes	Plants look sick and have damaged root systems.	Treat soil with Root Guard, Bromophos or Soil Pest Killer.
Mosaic virus disease	Leaves on tomatoes go mottly green or yellow and distort.	No real cure. Watch for its appearance and remove all affected plants immediately.
Onion fly	Damage to the neck of the plant which generally looks sickly. White grubs in onions.	Diazinion granules on soil around the infected plants. Rake in Root Guard or Soil Pest Killer when planting.
Pea moth	Mainly troublesome to main crops when moths lay eggs on developing pea pods, stems and leaves. The grubs bore into the seeds and give maggoty pods.	Spray with derris or fenitrothion about ten days before flowering.

Pea thrips	Very serious problem in dry weather when thrips feed on flowers and stems. Grubs feed on flowers and pods causing mottled patches on pods and leaves.	Spray with derris fortnightly and particularly immediately after flowers have set.
Pea weevil	*see* Bean weevil.	
Potato blight	*see* Blight.	
Potato scabs	There are several fungus scab diseases. Common scab marks tubers but powdery scab is more serious and causes swellings on tubers.	The soil is contaminated for several years once this disease has struck. Do not grow in the same patch again for several years. Burn all infected plants. Common scab can be ovecome by lining trenches with lawn cuttings at planting times.
Powdery mildew	Leaves powdery white substance on cucumbers, marrows and pumpkins in particular.	Spray well with benomyl every ten days for absolute protection.
Raspberry beetle	Brown beetles damage flower buds and dramatically cut crops.	Spray with fenitrothion, liquid derris or liquid malathion immediately.
Red spider mite	Can devastate greenhouse and cold frame crops leaving speckled grey–brown–yellow patches on leaves.	Spray with malathion, Sybol 2 or Tumblebug every fortnight. Spray plants with water in hot and dry weather, conditions which the mite particularly enjoys.
Root aphids	Root flies leave white powdery patches on roots. It causes stunted growth, mainly hitting greenhouse crops.	Spray with Bio Flydown, malathion or liquid derris every fortnight. Water soil with Lindex solution.
Rust	Affects leeks mainly, leaving 'rust' patches on the flags, which debilitates the plant.	Spray fortnightly with Benlate or Zineb.

Slugs	Can destroy virtually any edible material in the garden. It is easy to find, leaving nibbled foliage everywhere.	Slug baits are reasonably effective and liquid slug killers, like Sluggit, are very successful.
Spur blight	Purplish patches appear on the buds of raspberries and loganberries.	Thin out canes to avoid over-crowding and spray with Benlate every ten days.
Turnip gall weevil	*see* Gall weevil.	
Whitefly	Leaves sticky deposits on plant foliage. Mainly attacks greenhouse plants.	Spray with Crop Saver, Picket or Sybol 2.
Whiterot	Attacks onions, leaving them with yellowing leaves and white substance on bulbs.	Rake calomel dust in drills when seed is sown or in planting holes when transplanting.
Wireworms	Tunnels holes into young plants, sometimes killing the plant.	Rake in Bromophos before planting and spray Sybol 2 when plant is threatened.
Woolly aphids	Attacks fruit trees, leaving white fluffy substance on leaves, which curl and discolour.	Spray with malathion, derris, nicotine or pyretrum every fortnight.

6 Herbs, fruit and flowers

Apart from the ever-increasing range of vegetables that can be grown in this country, thanks to the never-ending efforts of the seedsmen, there are many other interesting items that can be grown on the allotment garden. There is always room to squeeze in a few fruit trees, or for a splash of colourful flowers grown for the house or for a tasty plant of herbs.

The successful growing of herbs and fruit can increase the take-home harvest of the plot considerably, both economically and by extending the range of flavours available for the table. Flowers can be grown for decoration on the plot — many gardeners enjoy a colourful front to their gardens — for cutting for the family home or, in the case of a small percentage of allotment holders, for exhibition purposes.

For all these separate items, the same rules apply as for the rest of the produce on the plot — they must be treated with care, kept free of disease, well watered and fed. An allotment with plenty of vegetables, a splash of colour from flowers, fruit bushes laden with produce and a neat herb section is a productive and highly satisfying plot of land indeed!

Herbs

This collection of plants can introduce new flavours to the kitchen, and the plants are generally not very demanding on the grower. There are hundreds of herbs which can be cultivated for their taste, scent or their medicinal qualities, but generally the allotment gardener will be interested in growing only a few which are useful for cooking. As many of them are quite small plants, they can be grown in a special herb block, with some of the bigger varieties being grown against fences or sheds. Details of some of the most useful are as follows.

Angelica

This is a tall plant which grows to about 2m (6ft). It produces stems which are cut from June onwards and used in chutneys and in the stewing of rhubarb or apples. Grow as a biennial, sowing seed in August to mature the following year.

Balm

This perennial herb imparts a sharp lemon flavour to iced drinks and cooked dishes and is easily propagated from root cuttings in March or from seed in early summer.

Basil

This half hardy annual is a useful flavouring for many dishes. When the leaves are pressed they release a warm smell of cloves.

Bay

This evergreen shrub is often grown as a standard for decorative reasons, with the dark green leaves being taken as required in the kitchen. It is usually grown from cuttings taken in August and kept in a cold frame through the winter and spring.

Borage

One of the most attractive plants, its leaves are often cooked like spinach or used in hot water to relieve sore throats. It grows to 38cm (15in) when sown from seed in July, producing the following year a beautiful blooming plant with sky-blue flowers with jet black centres.

Chives

Many gardeners believe that no garden should be without chives, a mild onion-tasting herb which is particularly useful for salads, soups and casseroles. It can be raised from seed or propagated by dividing roots.

Horseradish
This root is easy to grow and provides the hot and pungent flavour for horseradish sauce. Plant in February in well-manured ground in a place where its invasive roots can be controlled.

Marjoram
A perennial which grows to about 60cm (2ft) when sown as seed in March or April or from cuttings in June or July. It is a pretty plant which produces lilac-like flowers and is particularly useful for flavouring stews, often being used as a substitute for thyme.

Mint
This plant has a very invasive root system and should be planted in an old bucket or similar container sunk in the ground to prevent its roots spreading. It likes a cool, damp position.

Parsley
A favourite herb for adding flavour to dishes, and for garnishing. It thrives on well-drained land, and is usually sown in early spring for summer supplies, and in late June or July for winter pickings.

Rosemary
Another useful herb, rosemary is used to particularly good effect with lamb. It is a decorative shrub with lavender-blue flowers and is often grown in the shrub border. It is usually propagated from cuttings.

Sage
One of the most famous of herbs, it is used in soups, casseroles and in stuffing mixtures. It is a rather untidy plant which needs regular cutting to keep it compact. Although usually grown from cuttings, it can be started from seed.

Tarragon
The bitter-sweet flavour of this perennial is used for fish dishes, vinegar and sauces. Its dark green leaves give a very distinctive flavour.

Thyme

Another excellent herb for stuffings and for meat dishes, it is grown from cutings taken in early summer or from seed in May or June. Its flowers are known to attract bees to the garden.

Fruit

In even the smallest allotment, there is generally room to squeeze in some form of fruit, if only a few strawberries, sharing a row across the plot with six or seven raspberry plants. Strawberries are ideal plot fruit because they can be moved around the garden, whereas the bush and cane fruits need a special section of the plot. A decision to set aside a piece of ground for soft fruit will, however, yield many pounds of raspberries, blackcurrants and gooseberries for sweets and jams. Blackberries and loganberries, which can be grown against a boundary fence, provide a good wind break, a pleasing aesthetic border and some of the tastiest fruit it is possible to grow.

There are many other fruits that can be grown but, generally, apple, pear and plum trees should not be entertained unless the gardener has a large growing area at his or her disposal. Apples and pears can be grown on dwarf root stocks but they still need a sizeable slice of ground. Concentrate instead on getting the best yield possible from each square metre of plot and to do that concentrate on the following fruits.

Blackberries and loganberries

Cultivated blackberries and loganberries need strong supports and can be grown fan-shaped against the boundary fence. The blackberries produce larger berries than the wild variety, and will grow quite profusely in moist well-manured land. Use two-year-old plants, if possible, planting 3.0–3.5m (10–12ft) apart. They need very little attention apart from generous feeding of nitrogen in the early spring and a high-potash boost in early summer. Prune after harvesting, removing the fruited canes and training in the newer growths. There is usually only room

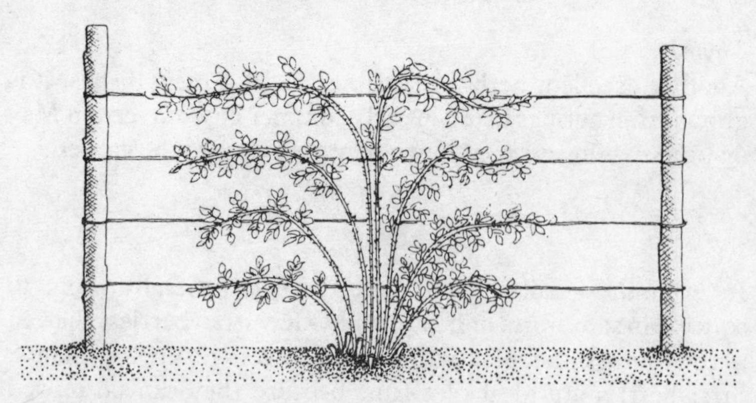

Fan training blackberries and loganberries; tie in the new growth after removing the fruited canes

for one or two plants but each one will produce between 7 and 9kg (15 and 20lb).

Blackcurrants
These quick-maturing fruits are very easy to grow when planted in humus-packed soil about 1.5m (4ft 6in) apart. The branches grow directly from the ground and the plants should be weeded by hand to ensure that there is no root damage from implements. Prune after fruiting to remove the old shoots. It is possible that the plants will have to be netted because the berries, packed with vitamin C, are a delicacy for almost every bird. Two or three bushes should be enough; they produce between 3.5 and 4.5kg (8 and 10lb) each in reasonable growing seasons.

Gooseberries
Gooseberry bushes produce probably the most prolific crop of all. For allotment purposes it is probably best to grow them as bushes, although they can be grown cordon-style. Plant two or three-year-old bushes and mulch well to help keep moisture in the ground. Prune in February by snipping branches by about 15cm (6in) and laterals to three or four buds to keep the bush compact and open. Two or three bushes are sufficient for they can produce between 4.5 and 7kg (10 and 15lb).

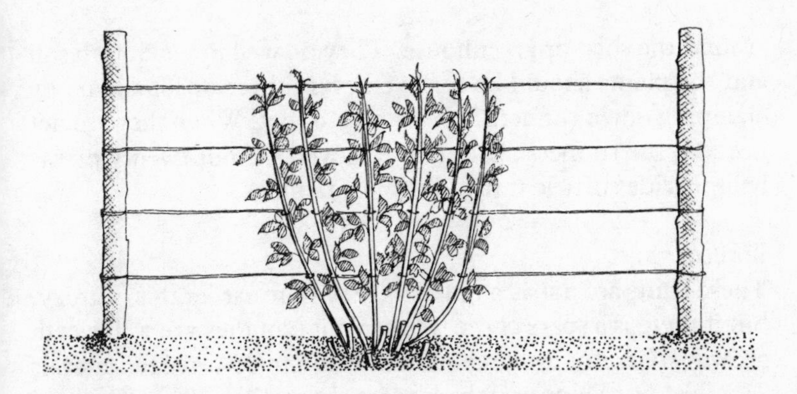

Training raspberry canes; tie in six new growths after removing the old canes

Raspberries

These are amongst the most rewarding plants that can be grown. They need wires strung between posts to support a row of plants, with six canes coming from each plant. Manure the ground well before planting and mulch with well-rotted manure or compost every spring. Plant the canes about 60cm (2ft) apart and cut back the canes to about 25cm (10in) of the ground. All they need, apart from the mulching, is a light dressing of sulphate of potash in March. After harvesting, remove every fruited cane and train in the new shoots. Ten plants will provide two or three helpings a week for the average family for about six weeks.

Redcurrants

These are useful fruits because they will grow on almost any soil, as long as the bushes are protected from high winds. The bushes should be placed 1.2–1.5m (4–5ft) apart, and all they need is annual mulching with manure and compost and a top dressing of sulphate of potash in spring.

Strawberries

These are a must for the dedicated gardener as they produce a large quantity of fruit, are easy to grow and simple to propagate. They can be grown anywhere, even in pots and containers around the shed or greenhouse. They do well in good, rich soil and the plants should be renewed every three or four years by clamping down runners into the soil to root. When they are not needed, the runners should be removed. About twenty plants will provide sufficient fruit for most families.

Whitecurrants

These fruits are not as popular as they were earlier this century, but if there is a spare corner of the fruit plot they are well worth growing. Careful pruning in the spring should leave the laterals 2–5cm (1–2in) long and the leaders about 22cm (9in). This will help to keep the centre of the bush open and produce highly productive sprays of fruit. Mulch in late winter and give a top dressing of sulphate of potash in spring.

Flowers

Flowers on the plot can be divided into three separate groups: flowers for cutting, larger plants for general display and smaller flowering plants for bedding purposes. They all help to make the plot seem a warmer, homely and more colourful place and, because the great majority are grown from seed, they are relatively cheap to produce, especially if a seed-swap system is worked on the allotment site. This sharing of seed or seedlings can dramatically reduce the price of flower production.

For cutting

Taking home a bunch of flowers from the plot can be as satisfying as taking home the Sunday vegetables. Some of the most traditional flowers grown on plots are gladioli, chrysanthemums, dahlias and sweet peas. These all take a considerable amount of time to grow properly — a rare commodity for a lot of people engaged in part-time food growing — so this foursome is usually grown for exhibition only. There are, however, much easier flowers to grow, and all of them produce lovely striking blooms to grace the diningroom table. They include asters, larkspur, clarkia and the two great old-timers, Sweet William and carnations. All are simple to grow, as are two of my own particular favourites, the rust-coloured rudbeckias and the annual lavatera, Silver Cup Mallow which, despite its name, produces glorious pink cups.

For general display

Many people like to have some of their favourite flowering plants around them down on the allotment garden, and in recent years I have enjoyed growing some of the larger flowers in a special bed on the plot. They have included foxgloves, lupins, Canterbury bells, the smaller varieties of delphiniums and one of my special favourites, hollyhocks. This group look particularly well if grown around or, in the case of the delphiniums and hollyhocks, fixed to the shed or greenhouse. They can, combined with clever bedding, really set off the plot.

For bedding

The work by some growers on bedding the front of their plots sometimes borders on an art form, with clever and complex mixtures of plants, foliage and colour giving an overall effect of quality cultivation to the visitor's eye. Bedding plants are grown from seed and are ideal for growing under a well-planned seed programme in the hot beds.

The choice of plants varies from the taller fuchsias and geraniums down to the smallest pansies and violets, allysum and lobellia, salvias, zinnias, marigolds in their many forms and antirrhinums. Once the seedlings are grown in boxes and planted out, there is little work to be done, the plants simply being left to knit together to provide a colourful welcome bedding to the plot.

7
Week-by-week summary of work

This weekly summary of jobs on the allotment is intended as a general guide for the gardener, listing vegetables that should be started, transplanted, fed or watered at the various times of the year. The guide can only be an indication, however, of what jobs should be done on the plot, in the greenhouse or the cold frame, since a lot is dependent on the weather. There is no point sowing seed by the calendar if the soil is cold, wet and unlikely to produce good germination. At the beginning of each weekly summary are suggestions for successional growing to produce food from the plot continuously throughout the year.

The guide starts, quite naturally, in January with the work for the New Year period. However well a gardener may have done the season before, the start of a new year is always a period of supreme optimism when the keen grower will make a daunting list of new gardening resolutions. During the dreary month of January the allotment may well be blanketed with snow or hard frost, or be a wet and sticky mess. Yet it is, like almost every other time of the year (December only excepted), a most important time of the year. There is always something to sow, plants to protect, crops to store, a path to lay or a new cloche to construct.

January Week 1

Successional growing: Clean away any dead or decaying leaves from over-wintering lettuce which could lead to botrytis disease and inspect all vegetables stored in bags or boxes for signs of rot damage. Remember, it needs only one rotten 'apple' to damage the harvest severely. Inspect all the frames and cloches for slugs and leather-jackets which creep under the covers in cold periods. Ensure there is adequate ventilation to control the atmosphere in the frame.

Onions and leeks: Growers of the large seed-grown onions and leeks like to start the New Year with their seed already sown or ready for the seed trays. They need a warm start in the greenhouse, in the region of 13°C (55°F), and should be sown in trays of seed compost as thinly as possible. Use two trays rather than overcrowd one, and water from the bottom by dipping the tray into a bowl of water with the chill taken off it. Leek growers who plant pods — otherwise known as pips or bulbies — press them gently into compost and keep them slightly damp but never overwatered. These must be kept at the same temperature as the seeds.

Plot preparation: Out on the allotment, place cloches on the land to warm and dry the soil for sowings later in the month, and clear the paths and sheds. Place an old bucket or box over the rhubarb crown and pile quantities of straw around it to keep the emerging stalks warm and dark.

January Week 2

Successional growing: More chicory roots can be brought into the greenhouse for forcing by placing them in 20cm (8in) pots and packing compost around them. Place another pot, with the holes covered, over the top and keep damp in a warm place. Seed potatoes should be bought soon, placed in trays and restricted to three shoots. If the ground is frozen, it is often an ideal time to wheel manure and compost onto the plot. During severe frosts give lettuce and cauliflowers some extra protection, if there is a spare cloche available.

Broad beans: If the soil is reasonably crumbly, sow early broad beans — Aquadulce is the best bet — being careful to sow them about 5cm (2in) deep in well-worked soil with the seeds spaced 10–15cm (4–6in) apart. Sprinkle a little peat along the seed drills to keep the soil lighter in this wet period.

If the soil is not ready for sowing but the grower is anxious to get an early row going, the beans can be sown in boxes in the greenhouse. Sow beans 5cm (2in) deep in boxes and this will provide excellent little plants for transplanting in March, especially if there is adequate ventilation in the greenhouse.

Kale: Pinch the growing tips out of kale plants to stimulate the leafy shoots lower down the main stem. Pull the soil up around the base to help the tall-growing plant in high winds.

Potatoes: Place the seed tubers of first early potatoes in a light, cool, frost-free place. Allow only two or three shoots to develop on each tuber by rubbing out all other growths as they appear. Keep them in the light, otherwise the shoots will become blanched and insipid.

Rhubarb: This can be forced very early by lifting some strong roots and placing them in deep boxes under the greenhouse staging with compost packed around their roots. Before taking them indoors, leave the roots on the surface of the allotment for a time. The frosting of the roots will help accelerate the shooting of the stalks even more when they are placed under glass.

Force rhubarb along by placing the roots in a box of compost, and placing it under the staging of the greenhouse, with a curtain or sacking over it to keep out the light

Seakale: Bring in the seakale which has been standing in sand or ashes against a shady wall or fence. Put these roots in a 15 or 17cm (6 or 7in) pot and cover with seed compost. Place another pot over the top, having covered the holes in the bottom of the pot with paper, as the crowns need to be grown in complete darkness.

Strawberries: A walk around the strawberry bed is useful in January to check for any sick leaves which could lead to fungal disease. Fork and hoe around the plants to break up the compacted surface to allow rain and air into the ground.

January Week 3

Successional growing: Lettuce and radish can be sown side by side throughout the year. Sow Sparkler or Scarlet Globe radish now and some Tom Thumb lettuce in a cold frame or hot bed. Mustard and cress can be started every fourteen days now in the hot bed, greenhouse or even on the kitchen windowsill. Sow carrots, radish and spring onions in a hot bed or cold frame, and make early sowings of peas and beans under cloches if the land is reasonably dry. Strawberries planted in pots, which have been in the cold frame, should be taken into the greenhouse now to bring on early fruit.

Cauliflowers and cabbage: This is an important week for those who love summer cauliflowers, one of the most difficult of all vegetables to bring to full and fruitful maturity. An early start is one of the main requirements for a successful crop because cauliflowers need a long, steady and uninterrupted growing season.

A sowing of All the Year Round, Alpha Polaris or Snowball in a tray, or even a large plant pot, will get the season off to a good start in a temperature of about 13°C 55°F. A sowing of Hispi cabbage, the sweet, pointed variety, will produce the earliest cabbage hearts of the season. Sow all these varieties thinly in trays or pots in the greenhouse, giving plenty of light and ventilation.

Peas: Sowing a very early row of peas in well-forked land. The round-seeded varieties of Meteor or Feltham First are recommended for January and February sowings, but do not attempt to sow if the land is wet and tacky. Even if the land is reasonably dry and crumbly, I like to sprinkle a little seed compost over the peas to help increase the chances of germination. Sow peas 5cm (2in) deep in rows 60cm (2ft) apart.

Potatoes: Tubers can be planted in large pots in the greenhouse now to produce new potatoes to accompany the earliest peas and the spring lamb. Place the well-rooted tubers in the bottom of the pots and cover them with compost, filling up the pots as the shoots break the surface until the pot is full; then allow the plant to grow and flower before picking off the small tubers in April or May. A dustbin with holes in the bottom can be used to produce a large number of tubers.

Planting potatoes in dustbins can accelerate the first new potatoes by at least a month

Fruit: As the buds appear on the fruit trees, the birds desperate at this time of the year for any fresh green material — will be out to strip them from the bushes and canes. Try to get some nets over them now. Raspberries can be cut down to within 15cm (6in) of the ground to make the canes strong for the season ahead.

January Week 4

Successional growing: Sow peas and beans in the greenhouse or in the hot bed frame for successional growing, and as a banker in case the earlier sowings outside fail. Sow thinly in deep boxes.

Erect wind protection, in the form of hessian, plastic or wooden structures, around crops that are particularly susceptible to biting winds, such as purple sprouting broccoli and later plantings of sprouts.

Beans: French beans are amongst the easiest of all vegetables to force in the allotment greenhouse. Sow about six or seven beans in a 20cm (8in) pot of potting compost and keep it well watered. This will

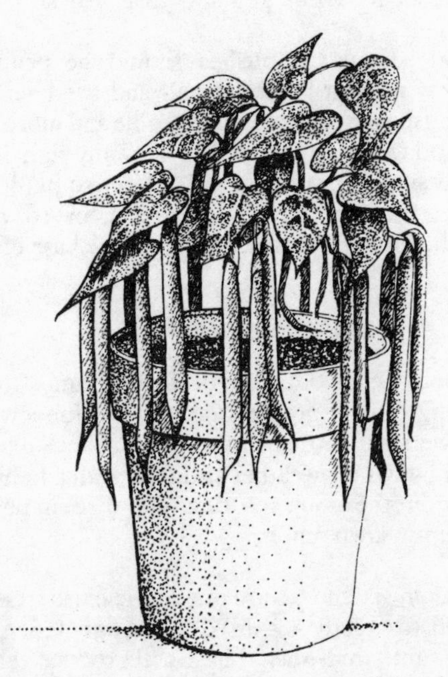

Dwarf beans forcing in 20cm (8in) pots are a useful early greenhouse crop

produce plenty of beans by late spring, and three or four pots can provide a number of useful pickings.

Clean-up: Any period of dry weather in an inclement part of the year should be used for cleaning up the plot and lighting a bonfire to burn rubbish and produce wood ash. Bag the ash as soon as it has cooled as the rain washes the potash content out of it if it is left uncovered.

Soil-feeding: Apply bonemeal to the onion bed now at about 140g per sq m (4oz per sq yd) as it can take many weeks for the slow-acting fertiliser to break down sufficiently to provide nutrients to the plants. Put Growmore on the beds for carrots, parsnips and beetroot to prepare them for later sowings.

Tomatoes: Tomatoes can be picked in the greenhouse in June if they are started early enough. Sow very thinly now in seed compost in shallow trays, the choice of variety being very much a personal matter. Alicante is my own particular favourite because it has an excellent cropping record, a distinctive taste and because it can be grown in the greenhouse or out on the allotment. Sow the seed on a windowsill at home if you do not use a heated greenhouse.

Fruit: White and redcurrant bushes should be pruned now by shortening the new growth by about half and the laterals to 2.5cm (1in) to keep the bush compact and manageable and more able to resist the winter rains and winds. If the bushes show any sign of losing their vigour, give a dressing of bonemeal at 140g per sq in (4oz per sq yd) and a much lighter dressing, more like 35g per sq in (1oz per sq yd), of sulphate of potash. Mulch over the ground at the base of the bushes.

February Week 1

Successional growing: Thin out carrots in the frames to reduce the chances of damping-off and prepare the seed bed for sowing sprouts, cabbage, cauliflowers and lettuce in the frame. Check over the spring cabbage loosened by winter weather and feed with a light dressing of nitro-chalk. Prick out the onion seedlings into three in pots and hand-weed around autumn-sown onions.

Artichokes: Jerusalem artichokes are one of the hardiest of vegetables and can be planted 10–15cm (4–6in) deep, about 30.5cm (1ft) apart, anytime from now until mid-May. These will produce very high tops, up to 3m (10 ft) high, which are cut back in the autumn. The knobbly tubers are useful for winter eating.

Brassicas: Prick out the cabbage and cauliflower seedlings as they become established. Do not let them get too large before moving them on into boxes, placing them very carefully into potting compost. The early sprouts — Peer Gynt is highly recommended — can be sown now.

Lettuce: Sowings now of Winter Density, Tom Thumb, All the Year Round or Little Gem under cloches will bring in hearts when they are still expensive in the shops. Sow rows of only a metre or so and try to keep up successional sowings every two or three weeks.

Onions: Ailsa Craig, still one of the most attractively shaped onions on the market, and Bedfordshire Champion onions should be sown in the open now. Sow in well-manured ground which has been improved by the application of bonemeal and wood ash.

Runner beans: Trenches for the rows of runner beans should be prepared as soon as possible, if this was not done in the autumn or early winter. They should be filled with well-rotted manure and compost and any other waste plant material to build up a well-balanced humus-packed soil. Incidentally, do not waste this ground; use it for growing lettuce and carrots under cloches. They will be fully grown and eaten by the time the runner beans will go out in June.

Fruit: Feed blackcurrants with general fertilisers such as Growmore. Tie in raspberries to stand the winds, and cut back the canes level with the tops of the training wires.

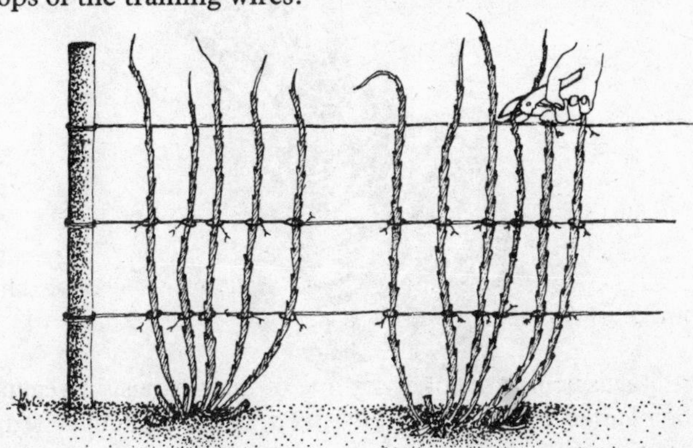

Keep raspberry canes under control by snipping off the tops level with the top wires, and then tie in the canes

February Week 2

Successional growing: Cabbages that were over-wintered in cold frames can be planted out. Check the asparagus beds, watching for slugs, and hand-fork out the perennial weeds. Sow sprouts, cabbage and mid-season cauliflowers in cold frames, and another row of peas — Kelvedon Wonder or Feltham First — can be sown under cloches.

Cabbage: More cabbage can be started in the greenhouse. My own particular favourite, Hispi, surely the best summer cabbage, Greyhound and June Star will all give good value if they are sown in boxes in the greenhouse or in a hot bed. Primo cabbage can be started under cloches if a greenhouse is not available.

Cauliflowers: Make another sowing of early cauliflowers in boxes in good compost — Snowball or All the Year Round are both ideal — to follow on the January sowings.

Celeriac: This is a turnip-like root which has a taste similar to celery and is a useful crop for winter use. The seed can be started now in gentle heat to produce plants for transplanting in May.

Celery: Some exhibition celery growers like to start their plants off in mid-February, but for ordinary kitchen use the sowing is best held back until next month. In the meantime, ensure that the trenches are kept weed-free and used if necessary for growing lettuce as part of a catch-cropping programme.

Celeriac — an increasingly popular vegetable

Cucumbers: Greenhouse cucumbers should be started now by sowing individual seeds in 7cm (3in) pots in gentle heat. Ridge cucumbers, for growing out on the allotment, should not be sown until March.

Shallots: One of the oldest sayings in gardening folklore is that shallots should be planted on the shortest day and harvested on the longest. That is a little extreme perhaps, but they do need a very early start and they can be planted carefully now with a trowel. Do not push them into the ground as this compacts the earth where the root has to grow.

Fruit: Mulch around the bases of fruit bushes and canes to stop weeds growing out of control and choking them. Check the grease bands on trees. These bands can be obtained from any gardening centre or homemade by smearing a piece of sacking with any greasy substance. This will stop wingless moths creeping up the tree trunks to lay their eggs on the leaves.

February Week 3

Successional growing: Start further sowings of broad beans and peas in boxes or pots for March and April plantings. Lift all parsnips now before they start producing new growth, and prepare the beds where carrots, beetroot, parsnips and other seeds are to be sown in the next few weeks. Sprinkle Growmore at about 140g per sq m (4oz per sq yd).

Brassicas: Sowings of later cabbage and cauliflower can be made in properly prepared seed beds on the allotment now. These beds must be well dug and completely weed-free.

Frames: The space left by transplanting the overwintered cabbage and the movement of lettuce should be used for another sowing of carrots for pulling when only finger-long. Sow Early Nantes or Amsterdam Forcing, 1.25cm ($\frac{1}{2}$in) deep and extremely thinly to stop overcrowding.

Melons: Sow melon seeds 1.25cm ($\frac{1}{2}$in) deep in 7cm (3in) pots of seed compost in a warm greenhouse, and water from the bottom by holding the pots in bowls of water until the pot takes up sufficient moisture.

Parsnips: If the allotment soil is drying out, sow parsnips — Avon-resister, Hollow Crown or, my own favourite, Tender and True. If

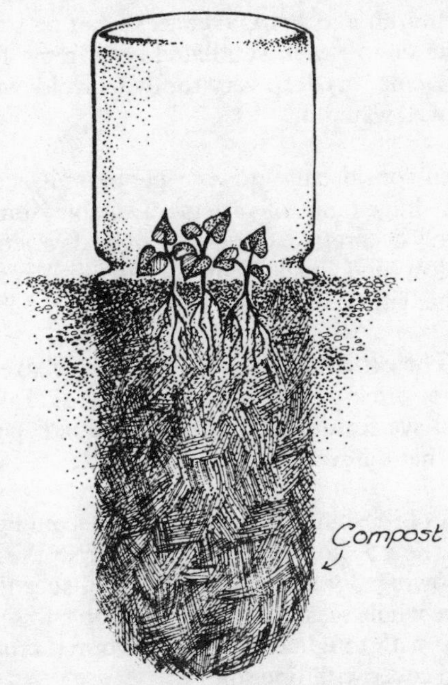

Parsnips are often difficult to germinate; place a jam jar over the seedlings to encourage them

you can spare a cloche, put it over this row because they are traditionally difficult to germinate in cold winters. If long parsnips are required, bore holes with an iron bar and fill with compost before sowing three seeds on the top. Place a jam jar over the top as a mini-greenhouse and rub out the two weaker seedlings later on.

February Week 4

Sucessional growing: Check every plant under cloches, particularly lettuce, for slugs. Asparagus beds should be hand-weeded now to remove perennial weeds. More sowings can be made out of doors of Brussel sprouts, early cabbages, lettuce and radish. Radish can be sown between sprouts and broccoli or broad beans because they mature so quickly.

Garlic: Plant the single cloves in a portion of ground that gets as much sun as possible, is well drained and not freshly manured. Plant the cloves 4cm (1½in) deep and about 12.5cm (5in) apart.

Leeks: Musselburgh and Prizetaker leeks can be sown out of doors under a cloche or in a well-ventilated cold frame for transplanting later. Sow 1.25cm (½in) deep very thinly to avoid overcrowding, and keep the row well watered.

Peppers: When considering growing peppers, it is essential to look carefully at the huge range of varieties available, some are edible and others are purely decorative. Choose F1 hybrid varieties and sow them 2.5cm (1in) deep and push them 1.25cm (½in) below the surface. Water from the bottom of the tray.

Pricking out: The earlier sowings of lettuce, cabbage and cauliflower will be ready for pricking out into trays or boxes. Take care to extract the whole root system of each plant with an old spoon or a wooden plant label so that the seedlings receive as little check as possible.

Turnips: These old-fashioned vegetables are becoming more and more popular again. Sow a short row of turnips across the root bed to start successional sowings for a constant supply of succulent young roots throughout the whole season. This is preferable to sowing a long row and ending up with tough and strong-flavoured crops. Sow 1.25cm (½in) deep and cover with fine soil.

Fruit: Feed blackcurrants with a high-nitrogen feed to give them a boost as the buds come into their own. Check any fruit in store for signs of rotting.

March Week 1

Successional growing: Sow a short row of spinach and more Alicante tomatoes for follow-on crops in the greenhouse and for planting out in the open in early June. Lettuces sown in frames earlier can be planted out in the open now. Sow more carrots, radish and parsnips according to the amount of land available.

Aubergines: These are best grown in the greenhouse, although it is possible to grow them under cloches or in frames. Sow them now — Black Bell and Black Beauty — in seed compost in 7cm (3in) pots and water from the bottom.

Beetroot: Beetroot, one of the essential ingredients for early salads, can be sown now as long as an early variety is used such as Boltardy which, as its name suggests, is not likely to bolt in the warmer weather. Sow the knobbly clumps of seed lightly along rows 15cm (6in) apart.

Carrots: Sow Early Nantes or Scarlet Horn if the weather is reasonably dry. This early sowing is helped through the inclement weather to come by a sprinkling of seed compost along the drill. Sow 1.25cm (½in) deep in rows which have been watered before sowing.

Rhubarb: As the forced rhubarb under buckets starts to send up shoots, plant new crowns in well-manured ground and feed the established crowns with a general fertiliser such as Growmore. Give them a good mulching too, using well-rotted manure or compost.

Swedes: Although not everybody's favourites, these are beautiful vegetables if they are pulled young. Do not, however, be tempted to sow them until May because earlier sowings can be hit severely by mildew.

Turnips: These are particularly tasty if they are grown without check, so a sowing now of Golden Ball, Purple Top Milan or Snowball should give the best results of the early sowings. Remember to have derris dust to hand for these seedlings because the flea beetle can devastate a crop within days.

Fruit: Prepare the ground for new fruit trees or bushes which may be planted in the next week or so. Dig plenty of humus into the ground and give the beds a sprinkling of bonemeal.

March Week 2

Successional growing: The Green Windsor varieties of broad beans (broader and shorter pods) can be sown now. Sow more lettuce — All the Year Round, Buttercrunch and Arctic King. More cabbage and cauliflowers can also be started in frames or under cloches.

Cabbage: A sowing of one of the top allotment cabbages, Minicole, can be made now.

Courgettes: These are productive and fast-growing vegetables. Sow under cloches now and the courgettes will be sizzling in butter by early June. Seeds can also be sown in the greenhouse in 7cm (3in) pots. The green courgettes are the quickest to mature, but the bright Golden Zucchini yellow skins are the most attractive on the plot and on the plate.

Catch-cropping radish and lettuce in the spaces between sprout plants

Catch-cropping cabbage between the potato mounds

Parsley: Sow this useful garden herb thinly and then run a kettle of boiling water along the seed drill to speed up a very slow germination period. Where can you get a kettle of boiling water? On all the allotments I have visited, I have always come across a gardener somewhere filling up a teapot with water boiled on a small gas ring.

Peas: Sow the maincrop peas within the next three weeks or so, starting with a row of Onward or Kelvedon Wonder this week. Sow in 5cm (2in) deep drills, and draw the soil very gently over the seeds. Water the drills before sowing to avoid the accidental dispersal of seed caused by watering afterwards. Remember, too, that the distance between the rows should be roughly the same as the height of the variety being grown.

Seed beds: Every allotment should have a small seed bed for producing leeks, brassicas and any other plants that need to be sown in a bed before transplantation to their final growing stations. Dig the land well and rake in a balanced fertiliser such as Growmore and bring the surface to a fine tilth. Dust along the drills with a seed dressing and pest killer before sowing to get the maximum production from the bed.

Strawberries: If strawberries were not planted out in August or September they should be planted now, although they should not be allowed to fruit this year. Take off the blossom as it appears so that the plants can build themselves up for a bumper crop next year.

Fruit: Mulch all recently planted fruit trees and canes. Check that all the ties are safe and secure enough to hold the canes in the March gales.

March Week 3

Successional growing: Mid-March is a busy time for successional work; more tomatoes, turnips, lettuce, cress and mustard can be started. Harden-off broad beans growing in boxes in readiness for planting out in ten days or so.

Sow autumn cabbages such as Winningstadt and Primo and start harvesting spring greens by cutting every other plant in the spring cabbage row.

Dwarf broad beans: One of the most productive of all the dwarf vegetables on the plot is the dwarf broad bean, a crop that is ideal for catch-cropping or for squeezing in a row on a small plot. Sow the beans — the Sutton is a good bet — 5cm (2in) deep in rows 30cm (1ft) apart.

French beans: Gardeners who use cloches intelligently will use them now for an early sowing of French beans. Sow two rows 30cm (1ft) apart and 15cm (6in) between them. Give the seedlings good ventilation in the later stages and the beans will be available in early June.

Onions and leeks: Onions and leeks started from seed should start their 'cooling off' period now by being moved into frames before being planted out in the open in a month or so. There is often a temptation to keep the onions and leeks going under very warm conditions, but this leads to soft and lush growth which is cut back when the plants go out in the open. The smaller onions, the silverskins for pickling and the White Lisbon spring onions for salads, can be started now. Sow in very shallow drills and simply cover with fine soil.

Spinach: Spinach is nutritious because of its high iron content and modern varieties make this very much an all-year-round vegetable. Try some with a sowing now of Sigmaleaf or Perpetual Spinach. Sow seed sparingly in 2.5cm (1in) deep drills, using only a quarter of a row so that the seed can be sown successionally at fortnightly intervals. Remember that spinach is a gross feeder, so feed with liquid fertiliser regularly.

Fruit: Feed loganberries, blackberries and raspberries with general fruit fertiliser or with Growmore. Strawberries also need a light dressing of general fertiliser with a fine sprinkling of sulphate of potash.

March Week 4

Successional growing: More French beans should be sown in pots in the greenhouse to keep up the supply of early beans. Sow a second batch of maincrop peas, using Little Marvel, Kelvedon Wonder or Onward. Grow radish and lettuce along the sides of the pea rows and plant a rooting of mint in a convenient spot, preferably in a pot to restrict its invasive root system.

Asparagus: The asparagus bed must be weed-free, especially of perennial weeds, before planting work starts because this is a permanent crop and the bed cannot be disturbed after planting. One-

Plant one-year asparagus in specially constructed beds, and spread the roots out before covering them with soil

year-old crops should be placed in 10cm (4in) deep drills with about 45cm (18in) between them. An asparagus grower has to be a patient person since the succulent shoots cannot be cut until the third growing season. People who want to grow from seed should sow the seed after it has been soaked in water for twenty-four hours in 1.25cm ($\frac{1}{2}$in) drills. Let the plants build up a crown for planting next year.

Cabbage: Some further sowings of Hispi and Minicole should be made now for following on the earlier crops. Keep the hoe working amongst the existing cabbage on the plot and spray fortnightly with an insecticide to keep pests at bay. Little holes often appear in small plants and this is confirmation of flea beetle infestation. This pest, which also affects turnips and swedes, can be eradicated with derris dust.

Carrots: Keep sowing carrots regularly and ensure that the early crops being grown in frames and under cloches are kept weed-free and do not become overcrowded. If thinning is necessary, water well after the work is completed and sprinkle Bromophos over the row.

French beans: Sow French beans under glass, in the greenhouse or frame, to produce plants for transplanting out in late May or early June, according to the frost forecasts. Masterpiece and Tendergreen are two good croppers but there are scores of varieties on the market now. If I have room in the greenhouse, I like to grow them in peat pots, the lack of root disturbance at transplanting means even earlier crops.

Peppers: Pot on the seedling plants into 15cm (6in) so that they can grow on in the greenhouse without becoming pot bound. If the

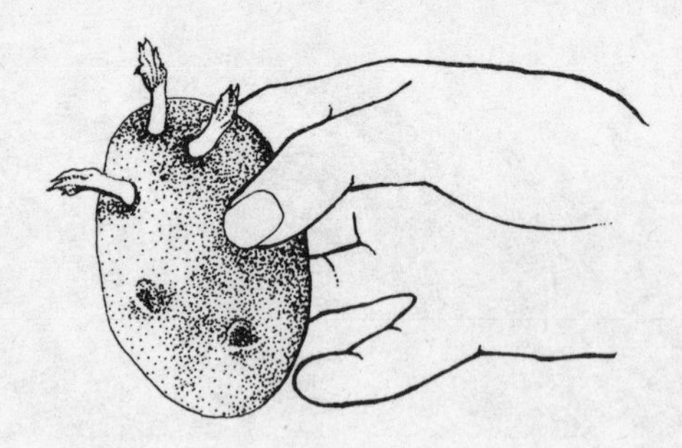

Keep potatoes in the light, and rub off all the shoots except the three sturdiest

greenhouse is cramped, they can be grown on in unheated frames or even on a sunny windowsill.

Potatoes: A harvest of potatoes in the first week of June is one of the ambitions of growers who are anxious to get the most from their allotments. There are two essential requirements for an early return — good rich soil and quick-growing early varieties. The land should be very well dug and manured in the winter. The best varieties can be found in a large group, a mixture of older varieties and newer names to the market. I plant Home Guard and Sharpe's Express.

For the first plantings, select the potato tubers with the best sprouts, reducing them to the three sturdiest before placing them in 15cm (6in) deep trenches. Plant them 60cm (2ft) apart and protect the tubers from excessive spring moisture with a couple of handfuls of peat or leaf mould. Fill in the trench and sprinkle Growmore over the surface.

Sweetcorn: One of the great strides forward by seedsmen has been with sweetcorn. Barring the most atrocious of summers, a fine crop of this extremely useful vegetable can be harvested. Sweetheart, Mellow Gold, First of All and Early Extra Sweet are just some of the juicy-sounding names. The seed should be placed singly in peat pots; if a greenhouse is not available and the cold frame is full, the seeds can be placed in their growing stations in mid-May.

April Week 1

Successional growing: Complete the planting of early potatoes as soon as possible and prick out the Brussel sprouts sown a few weeks ago. Sow cauliflowers thinly in frames for July heading and celery and celeriac for continuous supplies. Lettuce sown in the greenhouse in

Calabrese is an important crop for those gardeners who are keen to grow a steady supply of autumn greens

the early weeks of the year can be hardened-off and grown under cloches. More spring onions, radish and parsnips can be sown.

Calabrese: This green sprouting broccoli has become one of the outstanding autumn crops and it brings a welcome change to the autumn diet. Sow the seeds — Italian Sprouting, Autumn Spear or the dwarf variety Green Duke — in the open seed bed for transplanting in late May. Save some of the seed for successional sowing at the end of the month.

Carrots: By the first week in April the weather will be brighter and warmer and should be perfect for sowing maincrop carrots. These come in all shapes and sizes, I like St Valéry and Autumn King best, but I would recommend that people try different varieties and then take a decision on which suits your soil and family tastes best. Rake down the surface and draw a drill, just 1.25cm ($\frac{1}{2}$in) deep, along the row and then put boards down to stop boots compacting the soil where the next row is to be sown. I use pelleted seeds wherever possible because they can be sown thinly and therefore preclude the need for thinning. Dust the drills with Bromophos or Root Guard before planting and water carefully along the drill before sowing.

Cucumbers and marrows: These can both be sown now under glass. Choose the earlier fruiting variety for this sowing. Sow a couple of seeds in a 7cm (3in) pot of potting compost and take out the weaker at a later stage. Keep moist throughout their growing life.

Tomatoes: The early tomatoes should be making good progress now and can be potted into final 25cm (10in) pots, the border of the greenhouse or growing bags. Plant quite deeply in the pot so that more compost can easily be placed on top of the root system at a later stage.

Fruit: Spray raspberries with a fungicide to control cane spot and strawberries with an insecticide if there is any indication of greenfly or red spider mite in the patch.

April Week 2

Successional growing: Plant early potatoes now, and keep an eye open for the odd potato shoot from the earlies sprouting through the soil surface before the threat of frosts has gone. Make new sowings of turnips and plant out early summer cabbage. Place cloches over some of the strawberry plants to encourage the ripening of a few early fruits. Sow successional lettuce, carrots, radish and peas.

Beetroot: The bolt-resistant globe beetroot will be progressing well by now and will produce early crops if it is kept damp in dry periods. The long beetroot can now be sown. This particular variety is becoming more and more popular because it is so easy to slice for pickling. Sow 2cm ($\frac{3}{4}$in) down in deeply dug soil.

Cabbage: Feed the spring cabbages with nitrogenous feed, eg nitro-chalk, in very small doses to bring them quickly to maturity. Ensure that there is no gap in the late summer cabbage production line by sowing more seed, choosing from Hispi and Winningstadt for autumn and Christmas and Drumhead, January King and Celtic for the winter.

Cauliflowers: This is an important week for cauliflower lovers for sowings now can ensure that the lovely white florets are on the table until the end of Autumn. Sow Barrier Reef, All the Year Round or Autumn Giant for cropping in September and October.

April Week 3

Successional growing: Sow late-maturing sprouts, such as Bedford Fillbasket, for produce up to Christmas, and Citadel for buttons from

December to March. Sow winter cabbage, eg January King or Celtic, and salsify and scorzonera to bring a change of taste for late-autumn meals. Thin out the parsnips carefully, seeing that the soil is placed firmly around the remaining delicate seedlings.

Broccoli: Sow white and purple sprouting broccoli for winter use now in the open seed bed. The white-heading varieties, such as Nine Star Perennial and Early White Sprouting, are becoming more popular again and are very welcome when they arrive in March and April.

Chicory: Chicory seed sown thinly in a well-prepared bed now will produce the roots for next winter's chicons (the fruit of chicory). Keep the row well watered and dust with derris as the seedlings emerge to kill off flea beetles. The roots should be left untouched until they are lifted in November to be stored until January forcing.

Rhubarb: The sticks of rhubarb will be growing rapidly by now and will benefit from regular watering in dry periods; about 50g of sulphate of potash sprinkled around each crown will increase the potash content of the soil.

Ridge cucumbers: These cucumbers need a very rich bed to grow to maturity quickly out of doors so the land should be built up slightly by filling trenches under the planting stations with manure and compost. The seeds can be started in the greenhouse but must ultimately be thoroughly hardened off. If they are to be sown outdoors, sow three seeds, point downwards, on top of the trenches and cover with a cloche or jam jars. The two weaker seedlings can be removed later. The seedlings must never be without adequate moisture.

Runner beans: Accelerate the day to those bacon and beans meals by sowing now in pots or boxes in the greenhouse or frame for planting out in May. There are many fine varieties, Streamline, Scarlet Emperor, Achievement and Enorma being just a few.

Fruit: Spray raspberries with derris against raspberry beetle and use a copper fungicide against mildew.

April Week 4

Successional growing: Plant more onion sets and keep a close watch on the brassica seedlings in the seed bed. If small holes appear, dust immediately with derris dust to control flea beetles. Start to sow turnips every three weeks, concentrating on only very small sowings, to keep only a succession of young roots for the table.

Florence fennel: Gardeners who enjoy the sweet aniseed taste of Florence fennel should sow early so that the plant can reach an early maturity. Many people think its distinctive taste worth a place on the plot.

French beans: Those who sowed French beans under glass in mid-March will have healthy plants coming along nicely now. Sow another box for greenhouse germination, or under cloches, with the seeds 15cm (6in) apart and 5cm (2in) deep in rows 30cm (1ft) apart.

Kohl rabi: Sow this brassica in light soil in rows 30cm (1ft) apart.

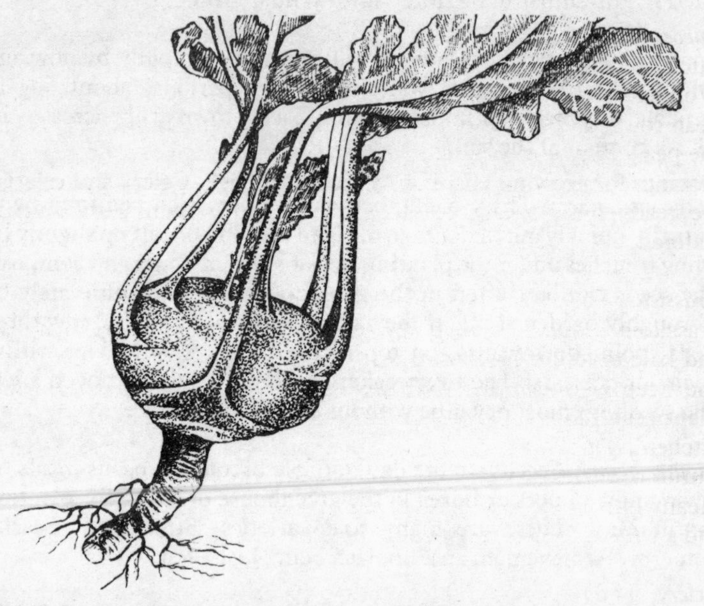

Kohl rabi, another increasingly popular vegetable. This will give a welcome boost to autumn cropping schemes

Marrows: These can be started now in the greenhouse or the frame. Try, according to colour preference, Green Bush, Long White, White Bush and Long Green. The latter is excellent for growing monsters for the heaviest-marrow classes. Sow in pots or boxes and make sure that there is a well-manured site ready for planting out in late May or early June.

Outdoor tomatoes: These play a large part in most allotments today. The improvement of strains means that plants can produce and ripen their fruit long before the autumn frosts. There are two kinds: those that have to be staked and have their side-shoots removed or the bush varieties. The former include my favourites, Alicante and Marmande. The bush varieties include Amateur, Tiny Tim and Sigmabush, along with another continental type, Roma, which grows long, fleshy and very juicy fruits.

Fruit: Spray loganberries and raspberries with fungicide to stop cane spot, and strawberries with a systemic insecticide against greenfly and red spider mite.

May Week 1

Successional growing: This is an important time for intercropping and catch-cropping. Sow radish, more peas and carrots, Kelvedon Wonder or Onward, if there is room. Plant lettuce between runner bean rows, and sow beetroot and turnips for pulling young between the peas. Plant early sprouts, 90cm (3ft) apart, and use the generous spacings for growing Hispi or Minicole cabbage. Celery and celeriac are ready for pricking out after they have been first thoroughly watered.

Brassicas: Early May is the ideal time to bring in another phase of brassicas: broccoli, second sprouts and autumn cabbage, calabrese and kale to follow on those already in the seedling stage. Sow thinly and keep well watered. Also suitable for May sowing is the Flora Blanca cauliflower, a large white-headed variety which is ideal for the kitchen. This will give heads in September and others, such as Autumn Giant, will produce food for the table in November. Meanwhile, make sure that the early cauliflowers get adequate water and a weekly feed of weak liquid manure.

Celery: The celery patch should now be made ready for planting in June. Make trenches 45cm (18in) wide with about 90cm (3ft) between them. See that they are not dug so deeply that the celery ends up struggling in subsoil. Work in as much manure and compost as possible as celery loves the moisture-holding humus in the ground. Sprinkle Growmore over the trench area to tone up the soil.

Chinese cabbage: These succulent vegetables are quick to germinate after being sown 1.25cm ($\frac{1}{2}$in) deep and copiously watered. They must never be allowed to dry out. They must eventually be thinned out to about 23cm (9in) apart. They can be used either as cabbage with hot meals or as a replacement for lettuce on the salad plate.

Salsify and scorzonera: These two root vegetables are grown in the same way as parsnips. Sow now 1.25cm ($\frac{1}{2}$in) deep in well-dug soil and water generously in the early stges. They should be weeded regularly and thinned to about 20cm (8in) at a later stage.

Strawberries: Feed now with sulphate of potash for the earliest fruits to ripen. Spray with a systemic insecticide against greenfly and a systemic fungicide against botrytis, except when the plants are in full bloom.

Fruit: Thin the suckers on raspberries, leaving those of medium vigour spaced about 15cm (6in) apart, and then feed with general fertiliser and mulch with manure or compost. Spray before flowers appear with derris or malathion to control raspberry beetle.

May Week 2

Successional growing: Sow the second phase of runner beans and French beans out of doors in their growing stations so that they can follow on the plants being brought along in the greenhouse. Tuck new straw under the leaves of strawberries to prevent mud splashings on ripening fruits. Thin beetroot and carrots, dusting after thinning the latter with Bromophos to protect against carrot root fly. Scrape hard compacted soil from around shallots to allow them to swell unrestrained.

Asparagus: Keep a very close eye on emerging asparagus shoots. Draw the soil up around them for support and place a ring of slug bait or soot around to keep slugs at bay. In dry periods spray the bed periodically to avoid drying out.

Marrows: Dig a quantity of soil into the top of a full compost heap or bin and sow marrow seeds. They will quickly germinate with the aid of the compost heat and, when their roots penetrate into the compost, they grow very quickly as long as they are watered well and get weekly feeds of liquid manure.

Onions and peas: Spray these two important crops with Dinocap, if there is the slightest sign of mildew, and all vegetables with liquid derris or a systemic insecticide if there are aphids — blackfly, greenfly — about the plot. This is vital if the plants are to realise their full potential.

Runner beans: Sow runner beans at the base of the sticks in the climbing frame. Two seeds 5cm (2in) deep should be sown at each station with the weaker seedling being removed later. These should be sown on one side of the sticks; the bean plants in the greenhouse or cold frame will go on the other to give the first flush of beans.

Swedes: The threat of mildew on swede seedlings will be receding now so sow seed 1.25cm ($\frac{1}{2}$in) deep along a short section of the root section. This is a vegetable that should be grown successionally so that young succulent roots can be pulled right through until Christmas.

May Week 3

Successional growing: Sow dwarf broad beans in growing stations, using the Sutton to get those smaller and yet really tasty beans. These are very useful for squeezing in on the plot when the allotment is getting a little overcrowded. Keep a close watch on slugs attacking the emerging asparagus spears and plant out later sprouts. As plants leave the cold frame, move in cucumbers and plant them on a mound in the middle of the frame. Hoe and weed around strawberry plants, giving a light feed of sulphate of potash.

French beans: Take off the cloches from the early rows of French beans and feed weekly from now on with a general liquid fertiliser. Spray with a systemic insecticide now on the basis that prevention is better than a cure, so that arriving aphids will be discouraged and probably killed immediately. Keep well watered as flowers and young beans appear.

Globe artichokes: Globe artichokes, the kind that send out fleshy bracts, can be grown from seed. Sow seeds in groups of three, 90cm (3ft) apart in a warm splot. Thin out after germination to leave the strongest seedling to produce the bracts the following year, and protect from slugs.

Leeks: Plant leeks for autumn and winter use. This is the easiest job in the garden; you simply have to force a hole in the ground, drop the leek seedling in and water. Use boards on the ground to prevent compacting of the soil by boots. Leeks prefer the ground to be well dug and fluffy.

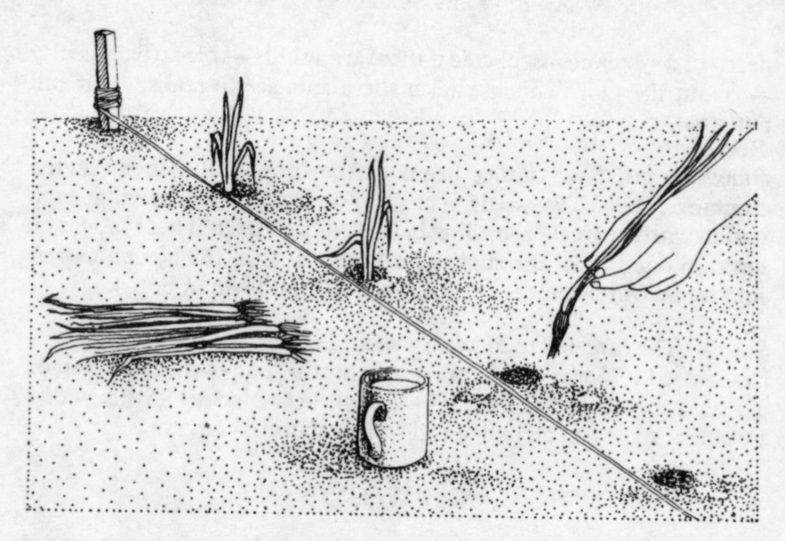

Dip the roots of leeks into a little water to gather them together before placing them in the dibber hole

Melons and cucumbers: These will be in danger of becoming pot-bound in the greenhouse and should be planted out on small mounds in the middle of frames. Rub out the growing tips of melons when planting and remember to restrict the side-shoots to four. Cucumbers should be stopped from growing too much foliage by pinching out the tip of each side-shoot as soon as it has two leaves. Pinch out the secondary side-shoots in the same way.

Sweetcorn: The earlier planting should be doing well in the greenhouse. For successional growing, sow sweetcorn in neat squares to increase the chance of pollen from the male tails falling onto and pollinating the female silks on the side of the plant. Keep the seedlings damp as they progress through what is often a very warm and dry period of the season.

Thinning: Various crops will require thinning now, including onions to 15–23cm (6–9in) apart, turnips to 12.5–17.5cm (5–7in), kohl rabi to 23cm (9in), carrots to 7.5–15cm (3–6in), according to variety, and beetroot to 23cm (9in). Water the rows well after thinning and pull soil up around the plant bases. Dust Bromophos over the rows to stop insect infestation.

May Week 4

Successional growing: Sow fast-maturing Early Nantes and Chantenay Red carrots for pulling young, and another row of French beans to follow the early sowings. Sow spinach to stand through the winter. As asparagus spears emerge, cut them a few centimetres below the soil surface with a sharp knife. Make the most of them because they can be cut only until next month when the spears must be allowed to grow into ferns to build up energy for next year's crop.

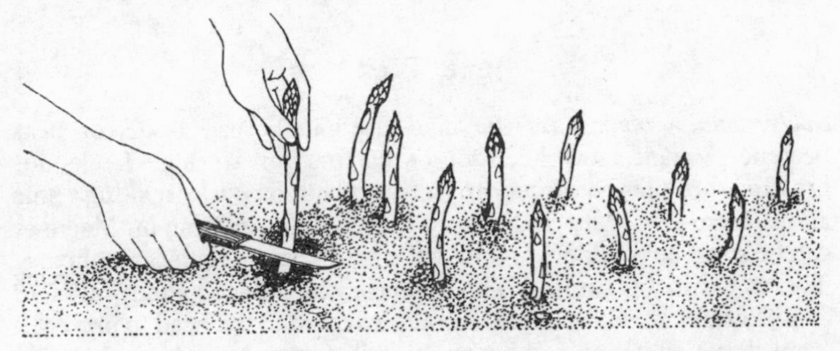

Harvesting asparagus; slice them off a few centimetres below the surface

Celeriac: Plant the March-sown seedlings of celeriac in well-dug ground which is free from fresh manure after they have been thoroughly hardened off in cold frames. Plant them 38cm (15in) apart in rows with 45cm (18in) between them. Make certain that the plants are well watered-in and get plenty of moisture in the first fortnight or so. Spray the seedlings with water in hot periods.

Leeks: Draw the soil up around the early leeks to help blanch their stems, and feed each plant individually with a light sprinkling of nitro-chalk or sulphate of ammonia. Water thoroughly with a hose pipe after feeding, taking care not to get splashes of the fertiliser on the leaves.

Peas: Be certain that peas are properly staked before they get too high and become damaged in the winds. Use hedgerow twigs, which are my favourite supports, or strings held along the rows with sticks or bamboos. See that the peas get plenty of moisture during and immediately after the flowering stage.

Potatoes: Continue hoeing up the soil around the young haulms on the potato rows, sprinkle Growmore around each plant and water in thoroughly with the hose pipe. Spray with Bordeaux Powder or a copper fungicide to reduce the risk of potato blight in the crop.

Tomatoes: Plant the young seedlings in their final position in the greenhouse to follow the earlier plantings. Tie the stems into the supports immediately so that the plants will grow straight and true from the beginning. Do not feed the plants until the flowers on the bottom truss have set and then spray with water to help the rest of the fruits to set as quickly as possible.

June Week 1

Successional growing: As the land used for broad beans or peas becomes vacant, sow beetroot or carrots for storing. Leeks for growing through the winter can be transplanted now by making a hole about 23cm (9in) deep and simply watering the seedling in. Marrows can be sown out of doors to follow the plants raised in the greenhouse. The hot sun of summer can damage the long-awaited curds of cauliflowers. Break a couple of inner leaves over the head to protect it from direct sunshine and heavy rainfall. Continue to keep the roots moist and cool.

Brassicas: Do not allow cauliflower and cabbage plants to get too large in the seed bed before they are transplanted. If they become too big the leaves are more likely to flop and struggle to become established.

Caterpillars: These will soon make a meal of the brassicas, so spend a few minutes on each visit to check the leaves of the plants. If you keep a close watch it should be possible to crush the eggs on the underside of the leaves or pick the caterpillars off as they appear. Otherwise spray with Picket-G.

Marrows and ridge cucumbers: Plant these out now making sure that they have been very well hardened off in the cold frames. Although summer has arrived, there are often some quite cold nights in early June and, unless they have been hardened off, they will suffer greatly. Plant 90cm (3ft) apart and rub out the tip of each cucumber when it has grown six or seven leaves. Train the laterals around the available land area to fill the bed. Pick out the tip of each leader as it reaches the boundary of the bed.

Runner beans: The hardened-off runner beans can be planted out now in their growing stations, just inside the sticks. Before planting, check

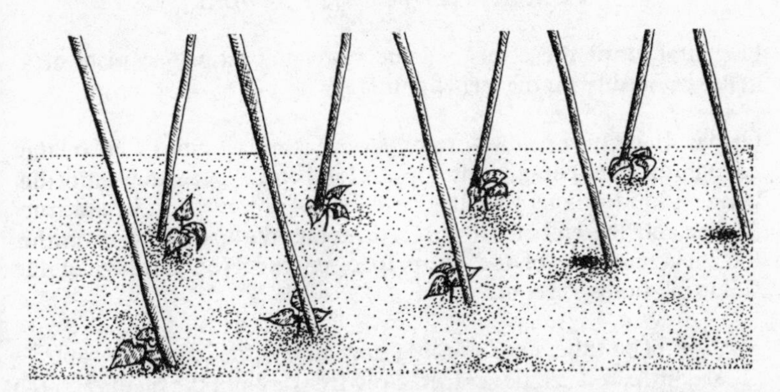

Plant runner beans just inside the wooden framework, so that each bean can link immediately onto the climbing frame

that the supporting frame is firmly fixed into the ground so that there is no danger of the frame collapsing under the considerable weight of the fully grown plants.

Sweetcorn: As there should be no chance of frost now, it is safe to plant out sweetcorn. Plant them in blocks 37.5cm (15in) apart to encourage pollen from a male flower at the top of the plant's spire to fall onto a number of female flowers on the side of the plant.

Fruit: Raspberry beetle can devastate the healthiest crop so inspect the canes regularly for any sign of small white maggots. Spray with malathion and repeat in ten days time.

June Week 2

Successional growing: Celery and celeriac can be planted out now after they have been thoroughly watered. Place slug bait or soot around the base of each plant. Sow white turnips between pea rows and make another sowing of runner beans and broad beans to follow on the plants already established on the plot.

Broad beans: Blackfly absolutely adore to suck the sap on broad beans. Apart from spraying with a systemic insecticide such as Tumblebug or natural killers like nicotine, the only other way to eradicate them is to pinch out the tops of the early beans. This pinching out will not only help to produce earlier crops, but will also cut out the blackfly's favourite home, the juicy young leaves at the top of the plant.

Celery: Celery plants will be ready for the trench now. Plant them carefully 25–30cm (10–12in) apart and water copiously. It will be a long time until the celery will be ready for eating, so plant fast-maturing lettuce on the trench top.

Onions: In early June the autumn-sown Japanese onions will be large enough for use, being ready for the kitchen between the last of the winter-stored onions and the cropping of the main onions in late August and September. However, do not lift the whole crop yet; allow the great majority of the bulbs to ripen properly. Simply lift the yellowing bulbs as required.

Potatoes: The tubers are swelling now and, if the gardener wants to cheat a little, soil can be scraped away from around the plants and the larger tubers lifted carefully for Sunday lunch, leaving the smaller ones to grow on for a few weeks.

Scrape away soil from the potato plants, and pick the larger tubers for very early new potatoes

Runner beans: Warm weather can seriously hold up the production of runner beans unless action is taken to help nature along a little. Water the bean row thoroughly, soaking the ground for at least thirty minutes, and then mulch the surface to keep the moisture in and the roots cool and to stop annual weeds smothering the bottom leaves. Help as well by tying in the growing tips to the sticks as they clamber up the bean poles.

Tomatoes: The earlier tomatoes in the greenhouse will be ripening now and the later ones, planted out last month, will be setting fruit rapidly. At this stage both sets of plants must be given adequate water, even if it means watering twice on very hot days. Feed with high potash fertilisers every week.

Fruit: Tie in the shoots of the blackberries and loganberries as they grow off the main stems. If they are not tied into the supporting wires, they can easily be broken. Mulch around the base of the plants.

June Week 3

Successional growing: Sow another row of dwarf broad beans and keep peppers on the move in the greenhouse, putting them into 20cm (8in) pots, growing bags, a greenhouse bed or even a sheltered plot bed. Feed with high-potash tomato feed as soon as the first fruits appear. Thin salsify and scorzonera to 22.5cm (9in) and plant out cabbages from the seed bed. Stop cutting asparagus shoots now so that the remaining spears can grow to maturity and build up the plant for next year.

Broccoli and kale: Plant these two brassicas now making sure that they are placed firmly into the soil since these vegetables, amongst the best value-for-money crops on the plot, will stand in the ground for many months. Remember that, like all brassicas, they are very susceptible to club root and cabbage root fly, so see that you plant on safe ground which has been treated with Armillatox or Jeyes Fluid.

Peppers: These plants will be growing well by now and should be in large pots, growing bags or the greenhouse bed. Start feeding with high-potash feed (a tomato feed is useful) as soon as the first fruits have set.

Potatoes: The tubers need plenty of water every week in a vital stage of their development. Remember, too, to keep the soil high up around the foliage so that the tubers are kept away from the sun which 'greens-off' a substantial percentage of the crop.

Spraying: June is a danger month for many plants and in a wet and warm mid-summer season mildew can easily set in. Spray the onions and peas with Dinocap and, whilst the spraying equipment is out, spray the peas again with malathion against thrips. Check over all the brassicas for signs of aphids or caterpillars and spray with systemic insecticides or nicotine if there is the slightest evidence of pest attack.

Tomatoes: All side-shoots on single-stem tomatoes should be removed with a sharp knife to keep the plants growing quickly up the supporting stage. Place straw under the leaves of outdoor tomatoes to keep the fruit from coming into contact with the ground.

Keep cutting out the sideshoots on the tomatoes with a sharp knife, to encourage growth

June Week 4

Successional growing: Melons must be stopped by pinching out the tips of the shoots one or two leaves beyond the point where the young melons are forming. Laterals should also be stopped at the second leaf joint. Sow stump-rooted carrots for leaving in the ground over winter, and transplant kale, broccoli and purple sprouting to their final growing stations.

Beetroot: To keep beetroot young and succulent to the end of September, there must be regular sowings of this important salad crop. Sow the seed now to lift in September for storing. Water the seed every day in dry periods; this crop needs all the moisture it can get to grow continuously.

Broad beans: The early sowings of broad beans will have set three clusters of flowers by now so the growing tip can be removed. This will not only accelerate the filling of the pods but also help to keep blackfly at bay. Feed once a week with a general liquid fertiliser, and if there is any sign of blackfly spray with insecticide immediately.

Marrows: The earlier sowings of marrows will be producing embryonic fruit by now, and by picking them when they are reasonably young the cropping period can be extended through the summer. However, to ensure that marrows are available into the autumn sow more seeds now — probably the bush varieties would be advisable — for growing on to the end of September.

Onions: To keep onions growing steadily, maintain an uninterrupted water supply to the roots and, once a fortnight, give nitrogenous feeds, either in the form of sophisticated feeds, such as Chempak, or basic nitro-chalk. See that the rows do not get overgrown with weeds as subsequent weeding can disrupt the root system and possibly encourage pests or disease.

Runner beans: Many gardeners will have runner beans reaching the top of the climbing frame by now. The tip should be snipped out to stop the plant climbing on unsupported and to promote growth further down the poles. Late June and early July is a prime time for aphid attacks so spray now with systemic insecticide. Water copiously as often as possible.

Shallots: Although closely related to onions which enjoy nitrogen, shallots should not be given a high-nitrogen feed. They prefer the more balanced diet offered by a general fertiliser which will promote good hard rather than soft lush growth.

Fruit: This is a dangerous time for raspberries which can easily be over-run by maggots. Spray the whole row of canes with derris to kill them off before they devastate the crop.

July Week 1

Successional growing: Sow Kelvedon Wonder peas for late crops and further sowings of spinach beat and radish. Nip off the top off the main stems of outdoor tomatoes that have four trusses set. On the cucumbers, pinch out the tip of the primary growth at the sixth leaf joint, the lateral shoots being stopped at the second leaf joint beyond the fruit.

Protect the summer cauliflowers by breaking the inner leaves over the curds

Brassicas: As the ground is cleared of the early crops, such as peas and beans, plant out more winter greens in the soil which has been enriched by the nitrogen supplied by their root systems. Great care should be taken when transplanting in this, the driest and warmest, period of the year. Water plants copiously in the seed box about three hours before transplanting, water immediately after planting and every day thereafter. If the weather is very hot and the plants flag very badly, shade with newspapers during the hottest times of the day.

Celery and celeriac: These two vegetables love water and cannot grow properly unless they have moisture at their roots throughout their growing season. Water with a fine spray for up to twenty minutes and use only a hand fork when weeding around the plants. Hoeing can cause accidental damage which may lead to fungal disease or pest infestation.

Root crops: This is the turning point of the season for root crops. It is the last chance to sow carrots, beetroot, kohl rabi, lettuce and dwarf beans for growing to their full potential. All later sowings will lead to small succulent crops, but they will be too immature for storing. The hot July sun means that the rows must be watered before sowing and regularly afterwards. Use a soil pest killer to stop root pests.

Sweetcorn: As the fluffy spires of the male flowers appear on the top of the sweetcorn, shake the pollen off so that it falls down onto the female silks below. Again, watering is important; if the soil dries out, the cobs will not form.

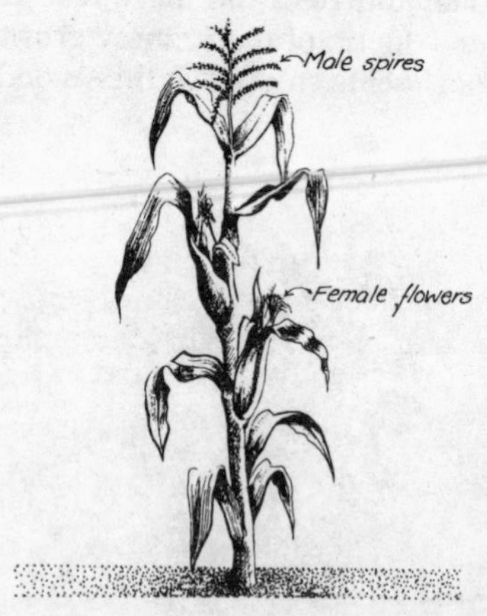

Shake the male spires of sweetcorn, and the pollen will fall down onto the female flowers below

Peg a strawberry runner into the ground, or, better still, into a sunken, compost-filled pot

Strawberries: Peg down strawberry runners to build up new stock for next year as the parent plants tend to deteriorate after a few years. Use a wooden or wire peg to hold one of the plantlets on the runners into the ground or, alternatively, into a plunged compost-filled pot. The latter idea is preferable because there is no root disturbance when it is time to lift the new stock. Cut off unwanted runners to stop unnecessary energy being drained from the parent.

July Week 2

Successional growing: Check regularly on the side-shoots of tomatoes; these are often sadly neglected when grown outdoors. Watering is essential too, not just for tomatoes but for celery, celeriac, marrows, pumpkins, cucumbers, carrots and onions. Spray potatoes with Bordeaux Mixture or copper fungicide as a precaution against potato blight. Sow more White Lisbon salad onions and Chinese cabbage.

Carrots: Feed all the carrot rows with a general fertiliser sprinkled between them and soak the ground for some considerable time with a hose pipe. Spray the rows fortnightly with a foliar spray — Foliar, Phostrogen or Maxicrop — to keep the carrots on the move. Cover the shoulders with peat and soil to stop them becoming green, hard and inedible.

Marrows: These will grow more profusely and certainly faster if they are hand pollinated. Take a male stamen and pollinate the female flower — that is the one with a mini-cucumber behind the bloom — with its pollen. Keep feeding fortnightly with a general fertiliser and, along with squashes, pumpkins and courgettes, make sure that they always have plenty of moisture. Spray with water in very hot weather.

The male and female flowers of the marrow; the female can always be identified easily by the 'baby' marrow behind it

Melons: Melons grown under cloches or in frames should now also be ready for pollinating. It is important to hand pollinate melons because nature can be a little slow in this respect. Fertilise all the female flowers — the ones with the embryonic melon immediately behind the flower — with the pollen from the male. Remember, as well, to pinch out all the shoots beyond the point where the fruit is forming, leaving just two leaves after it.

Melons benefit from hand pollination; strip the male flower and shake the pollen into the female flower

Peas: The ground around the peas should be mulched thoroughly to retain moisture and to smother annual weeds which can choke the crop and significantly reduce the harvest. Spray with malathion against thrips at least once a fortnight.

Runner beans: A dash of garden lime in the water given to the runner bean row at this crucial time of the year is a very useful aid to fruit setting. It helps to sweeten the soil a little and this, along with the syringing of the leaves and flowers with cool water, helps a far greater percentage of flowers to set into mini-beans. Mulching of the soil around the beans should be done as soon as possible, the ground being thoroughly soaked first.

Fruit: Spray gooseberries with derris to keep caterpillars, greenfly and other pests at bay. Water all bushes and canes in dry weather.

July Week 3

Successional growing: Sow yet more lettuce, this time concentrating on the mildew-resistant Avoncrisp and Avondefiance which can be transplanted in late September or early October. Spray brassicas with systemic insecticide to control caterpillars and aphids.

Cabbages: The first sowing of spring cabbages, one of the most important of the crops on the allotment, is due now. Choose well-established varieties such as my particular favourite, Flower of Spring. Harbinger is another highly recommended variety. Sow in the open bed remembering to water freely and regularly. Check the established cabbage for caterpillars and, when possible, squash the clusters of eggs on the undersides of the leaves. Spray with derris to be doubly sure.

Celery: A mid-summer check on the celery plants is essential if they are to be edible at the end of the season. Without adequate attention they can soon become quite tough and useless for the table. Remove all the weeds from around them, snap off all energy-sapping suckers from the base and give a thorough drenching with water. Potential problems from leaf spot disease or celery fly maggots can be guarded against by spraying with a combined insecticide and fungicide.

Onions: The autumn-sown Japanese onions will have reached full maturity by now. Lift them and, if the weather is dry and sunny, turn them so that the sun can ripen the undersides. Remove all the soil and loose leaves before storing in boxes in the greenhouse. Keep the other onions on the patch going well with plenty of water and weekly feeds of a general fertiliser.

Winter crops: The planting of sprouting broccoli, kale and the other winter brassicas should be completed within the next week. They must all be planted very firmly and heeled in to withstand the rigours of winter. Parsley, too, can be sown for winter use in a sheltered place. Later, it will be possible to lift a root or two for the cold frame so that parsley is available for Christmas and beyond.

Fruit: Spray blackcurrant bushes with sytemic insecticide against aphids and raspberry canes against beetles with liquid derris or malathion.

July Week 4

Successional growing: Plant out all strawberry runners taken over the last few months and water thoroughly before and after transplanting. Sow turnips for taking green tops in winter, and spring cabbage and lettuce for over-wintering. Use the ground cleared from potatoes for cabbages.

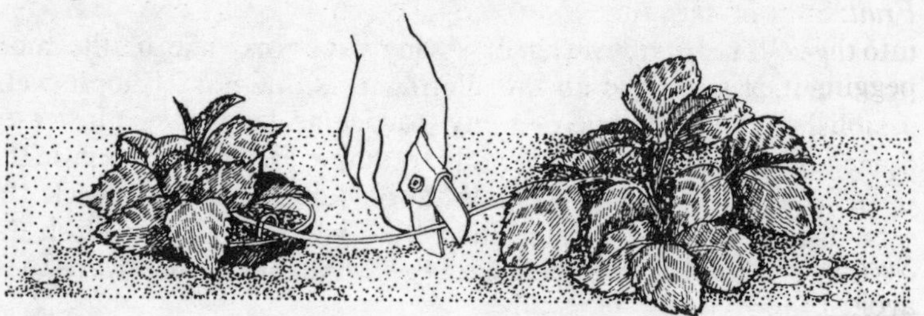

Moving the strawberry plantlets on; water the pot thoroughly before cutting the runner, and then plant it in a newly-prepared bed

Harvesting: This is one of the busiest times for harvesting, and it is essential that all the crops should be collected when they are reasonably young and succulent. Marrows, courgettes and cucumbers should be cut from the plants before the skins get tough, and there is nothing worse than picking stringy beans. They might as well have been bought from a shop!

Potatoes: Keep a close watch on the leaves of the potato patch for early indications of blight which often strikes in the warm days of late July.

Spray with Dilthane or Bordeaux Mixture. Feed with Growmore once a fortnight and weed frequently.

Shallots: Lift the shallots gently with a fork, remove all the soil and loose leaves and dry them on an upturned wire or plastic basket or on hard standings, such as concrete paths or patios at home. After they have been dried, place them carefully into boxes or baskets to await pickling.

Tomatoes: Overhead spraying of tomatoes on warm days not only produces the correct atmosphere for growth in the greenhouse, but also helps to set the flowers. Remember to pinch out all side-shoots to stop the plant becoming a mass of leafy growth and continue to feed weekly with high-potash feed.

Turnips: Although the latest sowing of turnips for mature crops has passed, it is still possible to sow a row to provide winter greens. Turnips, being members of the brassica family, produce very tasty winter greens in December and January. Green Globe is a good banker variety for this use.

Fruit: Start propagating loganberries and blackberries by layering tips into the soil. Lay a tip in a shallow trench and cover with a sandy soil, pegging it down if necessary with wire.

August Week 1

Successional growing: Sow another row of shorthorn carrots thinly, to avoid overcrowding and damping-off, in a cold frame along with mustard, cress and radish. Keep up the watering and feeding of melons, cucumbers and marrows in what is often the warmest period of the year. Take advantage of dry weather to lift shallots and lay them on hard standing to dry.

Celery: Start the blanching of celery by earthing up around the base of the plants. Wrap newspaper or thin cardboard around the stalks to stop the soil getting into the heart and damaging the edible section. The earthing up should be done gradually, drawing up only small amounts of soil at a time over the next two months or so. During this time there must be a close watch kept on slugs. Sprinkle slug bait or soot around each plant.

Protect the hearts of celery by wrapping cardboard or newspaper around the plants

Marrows can rot very easily when in direct contact with wet ground. Protect each one by placing it on a sheet of wood, plastic or glass

Endive: Start to blanche endive shoots by placing a flower pot over the plants, covering the holes in the bottom of the pot to keep the plant in absolute darkness. It will take a fortnight to complete the blanching process.

Marrows: Place a piece of wood, plastic or glass under the young fruits to stop them rotting in contact with the soil.

Outdoor tomatoes: Spread dry straw carefully under the bush varieties out on the allotment to prevent spoiling by contact with the ground, where they are an easy meal for slugs.

Parsnips: The roots will be swelling now and pushing the shoulders of the crop slightly above ground level. Cover the shoulders with peat or soil to stop them going hard and inedible. Hand-weed around the parsnips; one nick from a hoe can increase the chances of canker or other diseases getting into the roots.

Spinach: Sow the main batch of winter spinach now after soaking the seeds overnight. Sow very thinly in watered drills 1.25cm ($\frac{1}{2}$in) deep, and fill in the drill with the finest of soil.

Sweetcorn: One of the skills of growing good sweetcorn is to know when it is at its best to eat. It is so easy for this crop to pass its best

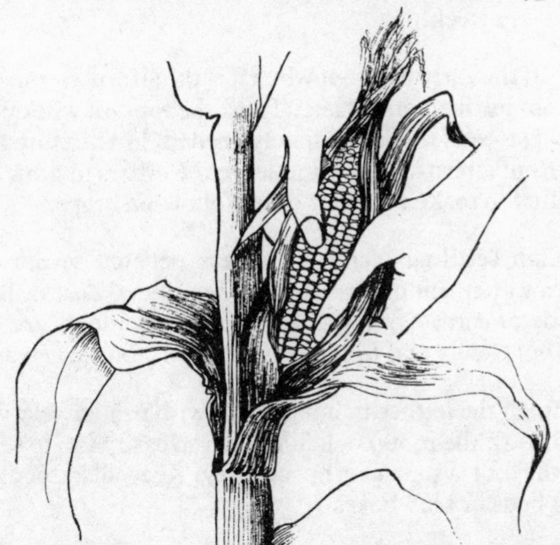

Test sweetcorn for ripeness by pressing a thumbnail into one of the seeds; a milky fluid indicates that the cob is ready, but a watery fluid means that it is not yet ripe

hidden in its green sheath. To check the ripeness, press a thumbnail into one of the seeds and squeeze out a liquid. If it is watery the cob is not yet ripe, but if it is white and creamy it is ready for the table. Continue to water frequently and give weekly feeds of a general liquid fertiliser.

Fruit: Immediately after the blackcurrant crop has been harvested, the bushes should be pruned. Shoots which have fruited this year should be removed to encourage the production of new shoots next year. Blackcurrants fruit almost exclusively on new wood.

August Week 2

Successional growing: Sow spring cabbage for late September transplanting and lettuce for heading in late October. Continue to water the runner and dwarf beans copiously and spray regularly with water to help the flowers set. Clip the bottom leaves off tomatoes to allow the sunshine to ripen the lower trusses. As runner beans reach the tops of the frames, snip out the tips to produce strong lower growth.

Beans: Keep all beans on the plot moist and continue to spray as often as possible with water to help the flowers to set. Feed with liquid fertilisers every week.

Beetroot: Lift the early beetroot when it is the size of a tennis ball to get the best from its distinctive taste. Twist the tops off without breaking the skin and store, if not immediately needed, in a mixture of peat and sand. Take out alternate roots and leave the others to grow on, unless they are lifted to make room for other follow-on crops.

Carrots: Thin seedlings carefully unless pelleted seeds were used. Soak the row after thinning and sprinkle a liberal dose of Bromophos over it to deter carrot root fly. See that the shoulders are covered to help keep out the fly and to prevent the tops going green and hard.

Lettuce: Mulch the lettuce in hot periods with peat or very well-rotted compost to keep the roots cool. They can so easily run to seed in mid-August if the root system gets hot and dry. Keep all lettuce plants well watered in beds or seed boxes.

Spinach beet: Spinach beet, a variety of the beetroot family grown solely for its leaves, can be sown now to stand through the winter. Sow the seeds in drills 2.5cm (1in) deep.

Spring cabbage: Even the best-organised and most-skilled gardener suffers failures, but it is vital that there should be no mistakes when it comes to spring cabbage. In case the first sowing fails, make a second sowing now as an insurance policy. A reasonable crop of spring cabbage is vital to any gardener who wants to make the best use of an allotment.

Strawberries: Prepare the strawberry beds for next year's crop by digging in humus in the form of well-rotted manure or compost. Sprinkle in 35g per sq m (1oz per sq yd) of sulphate of potash and 105g per sq m (5oz per sq yd) of bonemeal.

Fruit: Start to prune the raspberries as soon as fruiting is over, taking out the fruiting canes to ground level and leaving only six or so of the most vigorous new canes for next year's fruiting. Tie in the remaining shoots to the wire frame.

August Week 3

Successional growing: August rains can damage parsnips, so cover their tops with soil or peat to prevent them becoming hard and inedible. Tomatoes are often neglected late in the season but by cutting off the tips of the plant at the second leaf joint above the top truss the crop can be accelerated considerably. Feed autumn-heading cauliflowers in their mid-season with liquid manure and firm in plants with the boot. Sow onions to produce plants for planting out next spring, along with another row of White Lisbon onions for autumn salads.

Aubergines: Feed with high-potash feed and support the top growth with canes or a small frame. Try not to be too greedy, and restrict the number of fruits to about five so that they can reach full maturity rather than having about fifteen small aubergines. Keep the plants well mulched and watered.

Cauliflowers: Feed autumn-heading cauliflowers in their mid-season with a good liquid fertiliser and feed once a week from now on. Make sure that the plants are well anchored into the ground.

Celery: Spray celery plants with malathion to stop leaf miner infesting the crop. Tie the tops of the plants with raffia to hold them straight; flopping leaves can lead to damage and allow disease to get into the valuable crop.

Japanese onions: The most essential job this week is the sowing of autumn-sown Japanese onions so that these hardy little onions are established before the winter arrives. Sow thinly in rows 37.5cm (15in) apart, but do not be tempted into giving nitrogen until spring because the lushness produced by feeding is an easy target for the first frosts of winter.

Tomatoes: These are often neglected at this time of year. Continue to feed with a high-potash fertiliser and a sprinkling of sulphate of potash over the soil surface to increase the ripening process. Cut off the tops of the plants out of doors now to boost the growing of the last truss.

August Week 4

Successional growing: Although radish sown now will take a little longer to reach maturity than normal, it is worth sowing French Breakfast as a banker. Sow Dandie and Kwiek lettuce for growing in the greenhouse; the latter is also ideal for the cold frame. Earth up celery after wraping and tying newspaper or thin cardboard round to keep the soil away from the succulent heart.

Carrots: If finger carrots are required for Christmas, sow Early Nantes now in water-drenched drills and foliar feed the young seedlings so that they can become really established as soon as possible, certainly before the onset of winter. These small roots should be protected from the frost by having peat and soil put over their shoulders in late September.

Kohl rabi: Sow another row of kohl rabi to get small tennis ball-sized bulbs by the end of October or the first couple of weeks in November. These will have to be covered with cloches from the end of September.

Onions: The January-sown large seed onions should be ready for lifting soon. Lift the bulbs slightly with a fork and leave for a day or two to dry out. Then lift fully and leave them on the ground if the weather is warm and dry; if not, put them in the greenhouse or hang them in a shed in front of the window. When they have dried completely, clean the soil from the bulbs, remove all leaves and check for any sign of damage. Put damaged bulbs to one side to use first and place the rest on shelves or shallow boxes in a frost-free shed.

Spring cabbages: Fork over the soil for the spring cabbage that will be planted next month. Apply a dressing of general fertiliser at the rate of about 70g per sq m (2oz per sq yd).

Tomatoes: Late August can see the infestation of the tomato crop by whitefly. Fumigate the greenhouse plants with Lindane smoke and spray outdoor plants with systemic insecticide.

Fruit: New stock of gooseberries and blackcurrants can be built up by taking hardwood cuttings now. Dig a V-shaped trench out about 22.5cm (9in) deep and take cuttiangs from one-year-old shoots, about 25cm (10in) long, straight and cut just above a leaf cluster or bud.

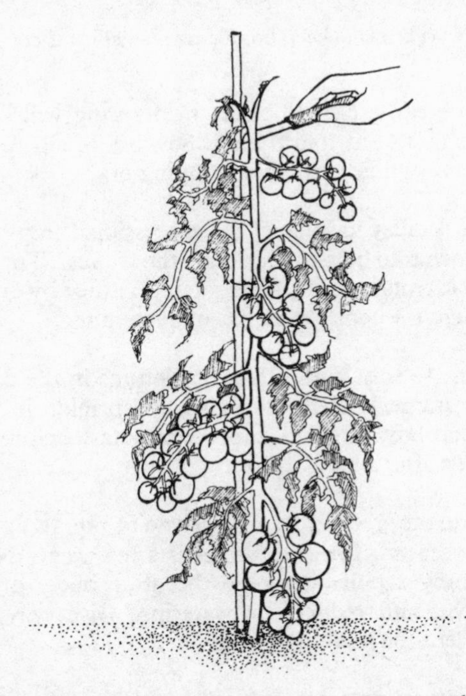

Outdoor tomato plants should have four good trusses by now. Cut the growing tip to promote bottom growth and to accelerate ripening

September Week 1

Successional growing: The first week of September signals the end of successional sowing out of doors. Work on in the cold frame only with sowings of endive, radish, mustard and cress. Most of the tops of the big onions will have flopped over by now. Pull them all down neatly, removing loose strands of leaves and soil from around the bases to help them to ripen.

Encourage dwarf beans to keep producing by picking them young

Cauliflowers: The earliest cauliflowers next spring will come from plants sown this month in cold frames. Sow Snowball, All the Year Round and Dok very thinly to avoid damping-off.

Cloches: If there is delay in some of the successional crops coming to maturity, use cloches to help to accelerate the harvest. They can help to bring on late carrots, radish, beetroot and lettuce by giving them protection through the cooler evenings of September.

Lettuce: It is time to sow Winter Density lettuce in the cold frame. Check that the frame is clear of slugs and sprinkle in very light dressings of superphosphate and sulphate of potash before sowing to replenish the soils after a busy season.

Melons: Melons in the greenhouse are likely to be rapidly approaching the end of their season. Fruit in frames is a few weeks behind and should be ripening rapidly, so keep the atmosphere dry, do not syringe the leaves and reduce the watering. Give only sufficient moisture to prevent the leaves flagging.

Potatoes: Start harvesting potatoes by lifting the tubers carefully and leaving them on the ground for a few hours for the skins to set. Use the smaller tubers in the kitchen and bag the remainder, preferably in sacks or strong paper bags, but never in plastic bags. These sweat the crop and set up an early rot. Burn the haulms immediately in case there is the slightest hint of potato blight.

Strawberries: This is the last opportunity to plant strawberry runners. In fact, if they are planted later the plants should not be allowed to crop in their first year. Plant in well-manured ground 75cm (30in) between the rows and with 37.5cm (15in) separating each plant. Set them so that the crowns are just level with the soil surface.

Fruit: Prune blackcurrants by cutting out old branches to reduce the size of the bush by at least a third.

September Week 2

Successional growing: Onion sets will have dried sufficiently now to be plaited together on a string, using their own withering leaves to make a rope. Once they have been securely tied, hang them in the greenhouse or shed for the winter. Ventilation in the greenhouse or cold frame should be watched carefully. The combination of warm sunny days and cool damp evenings can produce just the right environment for botrytis disease.

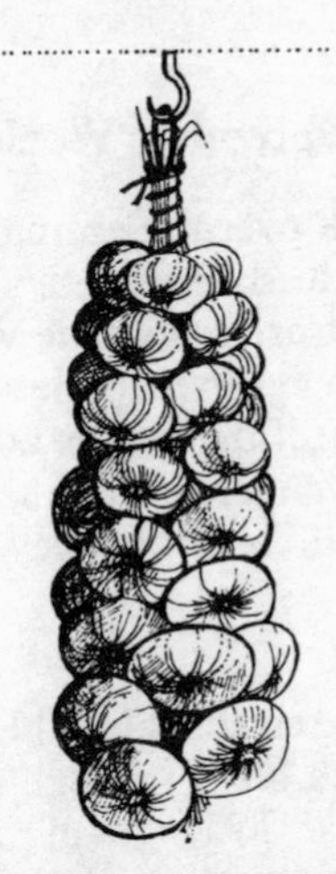

Store the onions grown by sets by roping them together — but make sure they are thoroughly ripened and very dry

Carrots: Maincrop carrots having reached their full potential, they should be lifted before they crack in the autumn rains. Dig them carefully and, if any get damaged, eat them rather than keep them for the store. Remove the tops and stack them in a shed or other frost-free place after covering with a liberal amount of peat and sand.

Cleanliness: There is a tendency at this time of the year to let general standards of cleanliness slide. This leads to annual weeds taking over, and this is where the old saying 'One year's seeding is seven year's weeding' should be remembered. So, do as much digging of spare land as possible, as well as hoeing around the brassicas in dry periods.

Peas: Cut the tops of the peas with the garden shears to shock the plant into filling its pods. Peas are often slow to mature by late September and this kind of shock treatment can produce some very useful pickings.

Spinach: The soil around spinach must be kept moist if the plant is to be stopped from going to seed. If there is an Indian Summer, soak the row and mulch along it.

Fruit: Prune loganberries which have finished fruiting by simply removing all the fruiting canes from the present season. Train and tie in the new shoots.

September Week 3

Successional growing: Fork over the ground for spring cabbages, but do not be tempted to add feed because this crop should not be grown too lushly before winter frosts. Give the winter leeks a weak liquid manure feed and continue to earth up the soil. Salsify and scorzonera can be harvested now, but if the land is not needed, they can be left until required. Transplant parsley to the cold frame, and careful planting and watering will ensure parsley for the table through the winter.

Leeks: Winter leeks will be establishing themselves now and a feed of Growmore will give them a boost through the autumn. Draw up soil around the bases to increase the length of the blanch on the stems and to give the plants more rigidity through the winter.

Outdoor tomatoes: The remaining tomatoes on outdoor plants will have to be picked now whether they are ripened or not. The green fruit can be placed in a window to ripen or used to make tomato chutney.

Potatoes: Continue to dig up the potatoes and grade them as they are harvested. The smaller and damaged tubers should be used immediately, the larger ones put on one side for chips and the medium ones for general use and storing.

Salsify and scorzonera: These two very similar root crops can be harvested now and stored, or left in the ground until required. When they are lifted, salsify in particular should be treated with considerable care, for the roots can bleed just like beetroot.

Spring cabbage: The land to be used for spring cabbage should be free from club root. This can be achieved by the use of Armillatox or by making holes in the ground where the cabbages are to be planted and pouring in the recommended dose of Jeyes Fluid. The plants need reasonable insurance against club root as they have to stand on the plot for a considerable time.

September Week 4

Successional growing: Carrots and beetroot that have been grown to full maturity should be lifted and stored in boxes of peat and sand. Smaller carrots, which are not likely to split in the autumn rains, can have their shoulders covered and be left through the winter. Lettuces sown in August for growing in frames can be transplanted and another sowing made for late winter.

Celery: The cold damp weather of late September heightens the risk of celery leaf spot and other fungal disease. Spray with a fungicide now and continue to earth up, remembering that damage to the plant can set up an attack by pests and disease.

Parsley: Transplant some parsley plants to the cold frame about 15cm (6in) apart. Careful cultivation and harvesting will make parsley available throughout the year.

Rhubarb: The long rhubarb season that started with forcing in January is over. Clear away the dead leaves around the roots, and as soon as the frost touches the stems remove them and lightly fork over the ground around the crowns.

Runner beans: Do not neglect runner beans; keep them fed and watered throughout early October, and they will continue to provide nice stringless beans as long as they are picked young. Spray with a foliar feed once a week to help the beans in their final weeks.

Shallots: During spells of inclement weather when work is impossible on the plot, spend time sorting out the shallots in store. Select medium-sized bulbs that are firm and nicely ripened for planting next year. Store them somewhere dry, cool and frost-free.

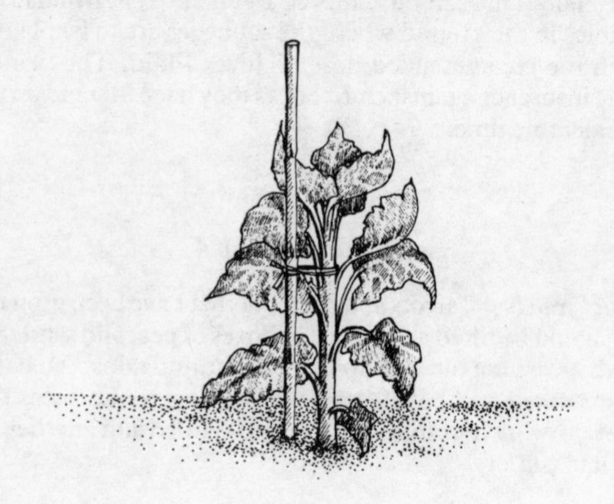

Stake the sprout plants securely to protect them against winter winds

Sprouts: Stake the sprouts with sticks or strong bamboos and tie up with raffia. Mound soil up around the base of the stems to give the plant extra rigidity in the soil to protect the root system of the plant from rocking in the strong winter winds.

October Week 1

Successional growing: The late sowings of French beans should be covered with cloches now to protect them from the cool nights and the possibility of frost. Earth up celery, probably for the last time. Plant out spring cabbage and firm each plant well into the ground.

Brassicas: A close inspection of the brassicas, including turnips and swedes, is vital now to ensure that there is no infestation of mealy aphids which often strike in early October. Spray with a systemic insecticide; swedes will also benefit from a fungicidal spray to reduce the fear of mildew.

Digging: As the allotment garden is cleared of autumn-maturing vegetables, dig as much as the weather will allow. If the soil is particularly heavy, ridge the land by constructing a series of lumps across the plot so that the wind, rain and frost have more surface area of ground to break down. Dig manure and compost into the onion and leek beds and give a light dressing of slag.

Onion sets: An interesting recent advance in vegetable growing is the autumn-planted onion set. These sets should be planted now in well-drained land with Growmore applied a week or so before. Plant them carefully by trowel about 15cm (6in) apart. Do not be tempted to feed with nitrogenous feed because it will only produce lush growth which is an easy target for frost.

Sprouts: Remove all the yellowing bottom leaves on the sprout plants and put them on the compost heap. This will allow light and air in around the stems and developing buttons.

October Week 2

Successional growing: Dig green manure crops into the soil making sure that all leaves are dug in properly. Sprinkle the land with a nitrogen feed, such as nitro-chalk, to help to accelerate decomposition. Stake up sprouts against the wind and remove yellowing leaves to allow air to circulate and reduce the chance of fungal disease.

Endive: Although considered quite hardy, some endive should be taken into a cold frame to ensure supplies in the severest winter. If there are spare cloches available, they can be used to cover some of the endive plants left in the open.

Kohl rabi: When these plants are about the size of tennis balls, lift them for eating as required. If there are still some smaller ones struggling to reach maturity, place a cloche over them to protect them from frost.

Lettuce: When planting the winter varieties sown last month, remember to take particular care that the seed leaves are not buried. This can give rise to damping-off which can destroy the crop.

Mint: A supply of mint is often most welcome in the winter months, so lift a few roots now, lay them on a light compost in a deep tray or box and cover with a couple of centimetres of compost. Water regularly and place in the greenhouse and it will soon produce enough leaves to give mint for sauces.

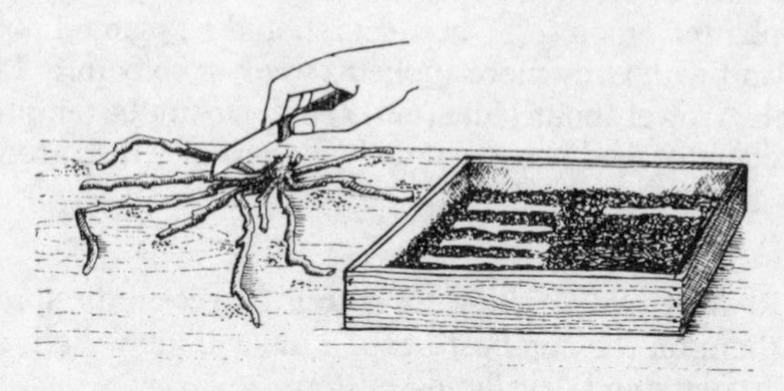

Mint can be brought to the table very early by taking root cuttings now, and placing them in a box of compost

Slugs: On warm autumn evenings slugs are often on the rampage. Put down slug bait or set up slug traps, such as the beer trap, to kill off the population before they attack spring plantings.

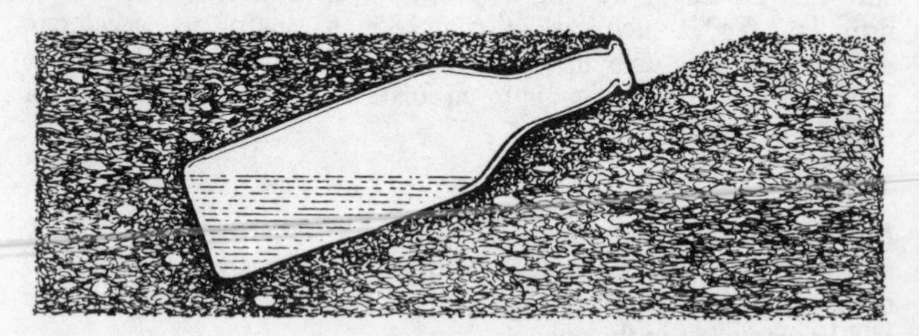

Slugs love beer; bury a bottle half-filled with beer in the soil, and they will crawl in and fall to the bottom

October Week 3

Successional growing: As the weather gets colder the slugs will be trying to get into the frames, cloches and greenhouses. Protect lettuce with bait or soot and clear away rubbish heaps and other potential slug havens. Lift a good supply of turnips and store in a pile in a frost-free shed. Cut off the tops and cover with straw, leaving others on the plot to produce greens in the depths of winter.

Asparagus: Cut down and clear the tops of the asparagus plants before the berries drop to the ground. Hand-weed out all the perennial weeds and give the whole bed a good mulching from the compost heap.

Cauliflowers: As the first severe frosts of late autumn threaten, check that all the cauliflowers with late autumn curds have an outer leaf bent over them. This is just enough protection to allow the curds to remain hard and crisp.

Sprouts: The sprouts have been in the ground for some considerable time now, and would benefit from a general feed such as Growmore or other general fertiliser to tone up the soil for the winter. Check around the leaves for signs of mealy bugs or even late caterpillars which can sometimes be a nuisance in warm autumns.

Turnips: Thin the turnip rows and start pulling the young roots when they are really no larger than a tennis ball. If there are still mature roots in other rows, lift them now and, after cutting off the top growths, place in a shed or under greenhouse staging.

October Week 4

Successional growing: Seakale beet helps to fill the gap in the supply of fresh vegetables in late October, but only take a few leaves at a time from each plant to avoid weakening the plants unnecessarily. Seakale roots can also be lifted and the crowns stored in sand until they are needed for forcing. Cut the tops from celeriac plants, lift the round bulbous roots and store in damp sand in a shed.

Brassicas: Walk round the entire brassica family on the plot before winter finally sets in, remove every decaying leaf and firm down the plants in the ground with the heel of the boot. Check the ties on the sprout stakes and spray for the last time with a systemic spray.

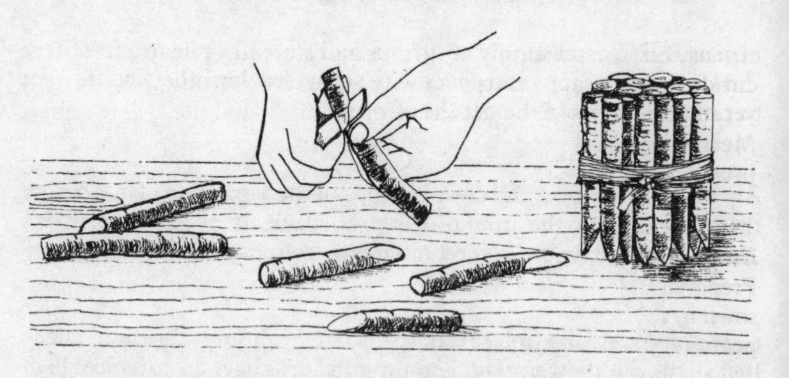

Seakale roots can now be lifted and the crowns stored in sand, ready for spring planting

Celeriac: Do not let the roots grow hard and woody by leaving them out too long. Pull now before the early frost, cutting off the leaves and storing in damp sand in the shed.

Celery: Complete the earthing up of the celery crop and spray with Bordeaux Mixture or a fungicide to check the threat of rust. Although late in the year, watch out for slugs.

Fertilisers: October is the ideal time to apply slow-acting fertilisers such as basic slag and bonemeal. Work out, on the crop rotation plan, where the brassicas are to be planted next year and cover with a liberal dose of garden lime.

Glass: Clean the glass in the greenhouse, inside and out, as well as the cold frames and the glass cloches, so that winter crops get all the light available. The transmission of light is one of the most important factors in plant growth under glass.

November Week 1

Successional growing: Lift and store Jerusalem artichokes in the same way as potatoes. Check sprouts again for yellow leaves and ensure that all the tall-growing brassicas are firmly anchored to the soil. Sow another row of the round seed peas, such as Feltham First or Meteor, using a cloche if possible.

Artichokes: The stems of Chinese and Jerusalem artichokes should be cut down almost to ground level. The tubers need not be harvested yet, though; they are better left in the ground until they are required. Meanwhile, remove all the flower stems from the globe artichokes and protect the crowns from frost with heavy mulching.

Broad beans: It is virtually the start of another year for broad beans. Prepare the ground for hardy beans such as Aquadulce which can be sown in the next week or so. Dig the row deep and sprinkle in a little peat to lighten the ground.

Celery: Continue to earth up the celery. If there are warnings of severe frost, try to protect the tops by wrapping polythene or straw around them. Although it is late in the year, continue to protect the celery sticks from slugs with slug bait or rings of soot around the plants.

Chicory can be forced now to produce chicons for the New Year

Chicory: Lift chicory roots with the greatest of care by cutting down the leaves to within 2.5cm (1in) of the top of the crowns. Pack the roots carefully, crown upwards, in boxes or pots with a mixture of peat and soil. Moisten the boxes or pots and place them in a dark place for forcing, under the greenhouse staging or under the bed of the spare bedroom, if necessary.

November Week 2

Successional growing: Scorzonera and salsify should be lifted by now, taking care not to damage the salsify because it can bleed like beetroot. Broad beans (Aqualdulce) can be sown again now to double the chances of getting a row of beans through the winter.

Broad beans: Sow Aqualdulce broad beans for the earliest crops next year; the young plants need time to become established before the worst of the winter sets in. Sow 5cm (2in) deep in a double row with about 30cm (1ft) between. When the seedlings break through, pull the soil up around them to anchor them firmly into the row.

Peas: Round-seeded peas, such as Meteor or Feltham First, should be sown within the next week, although it is absolutely vital that the ground should be well drained and reasonably dry when sowing takes place. This is where cloches can come into service again; protection on the pea rows now considerably accelerates the appearance of the crops early next spring.

Rhubarb and seakale: These can both be lifted for forcing anytime now. It is advisable to leave the rhubarb on the ground for a week or so to be touched by frost before being taken into the heated greenhouse next month when the onions are started. Seakale can be forced by pressing roots into compost, just as chicory is forced and blanched, and placing in the dark under the greenhouse staging.

Runner beans: Clear away the beans but leave the root systems intact in the ground for a few weeks to enable the nitrogen from the root nodules to be transferred into the ground.

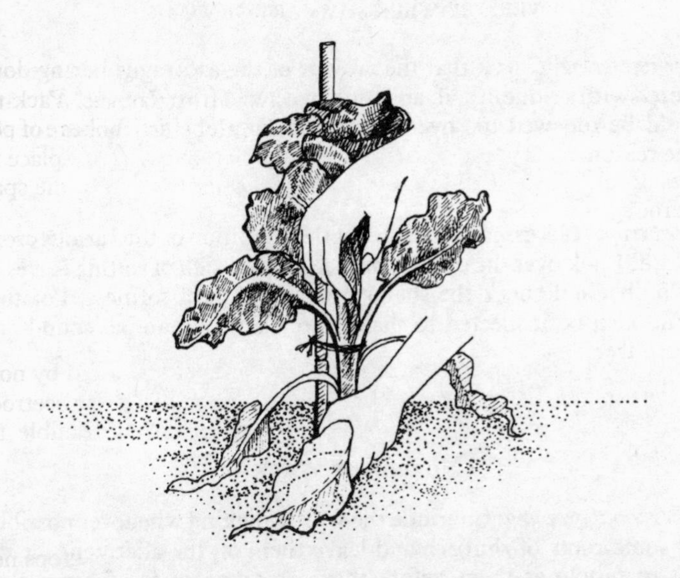

All yellowing leaves must be removed from sprout plants to keep them healthy and disease-free

Sprouts: If some Brussel sprout plants are slow to develop buttons, remove the tops of the plant to shock it into development. Remove all the yellowing leaves and weed regularly around the plants. Draw soil up around the stems again to hold the stalks firmly in place, and check that the stakes are secure.

November Week 3

Successional growing: Hand-hoe between the winter lettuces when the soil is reasonably dry to allow rain and air to penetrate. Remove yellowing leaves from any crops in cold frames and ensure that there is adequate ventilation even in cold spells.

Onions: Weed around the autumn-sown onions before they get smothered with annual weeds. Be careful, though, not to expose the roots to the frost and do not feed at all. Wait until spring to start the nitrogen feeding programme.

Over-wintering: Check that the crowns of the asparagus bed are well covered with a ridge of soil, and mulch to avoid frost damage. Mulches should be renewed too over the crowns of globe artichokes for the same reason.

Stored crops: It is essential to inspect the condition of the various crops in store. Look over the onions for the slightest sign of rotting leaves or soft bulbs, and check the shallots for any sign of softness. Potatoes should also be inspected to make sure that they are all sound and disease-free.

November Week 4

Successional growing: Continue the winter digging whenever possible. Lift some roots of rhubarb and leave them on the allotment for the frost to nibble at them before they are taken in for forcing after Christmas.

Lettuce: Lettuce seedlings sown earlier in the greenhouse should be thinned out to about 23cm (9in), given plenty of ventilation and only moderate amounts of moisture.

Parsnips and horseradish: These are two of the hardiest vegetables on the plot and they can withstand the severest weather. However, when the ground is frozen hard, digging them up when required can be a thankless task, so dig some up now, cut off the tops and leave them in the soil at the side of the path for easy access.

Runner beans: The trench for next year's runner beans should be filled with manure, compost and other household waste material as soon as possible for decomposition to start in earnest. Use the soil on top of the trench for planting early spring lettuce under cloches.

December

If there is an ideal time for a gardener to go on holiday it is the first two weeks of December. There is little to do except dig the ground if the weather is kind, clean out the greenhouse and shed and ventilate the cold frames. Towards the end of the month wash and disinfect all your trays and pots ready for the start of another year, and some people like to sow their leeks and onions in the last couple of days of the year.

On 31 December there is one other job to do, the last in a very busy and productive year. Make a resolution to try to get even more from the allotment in the year ahead!

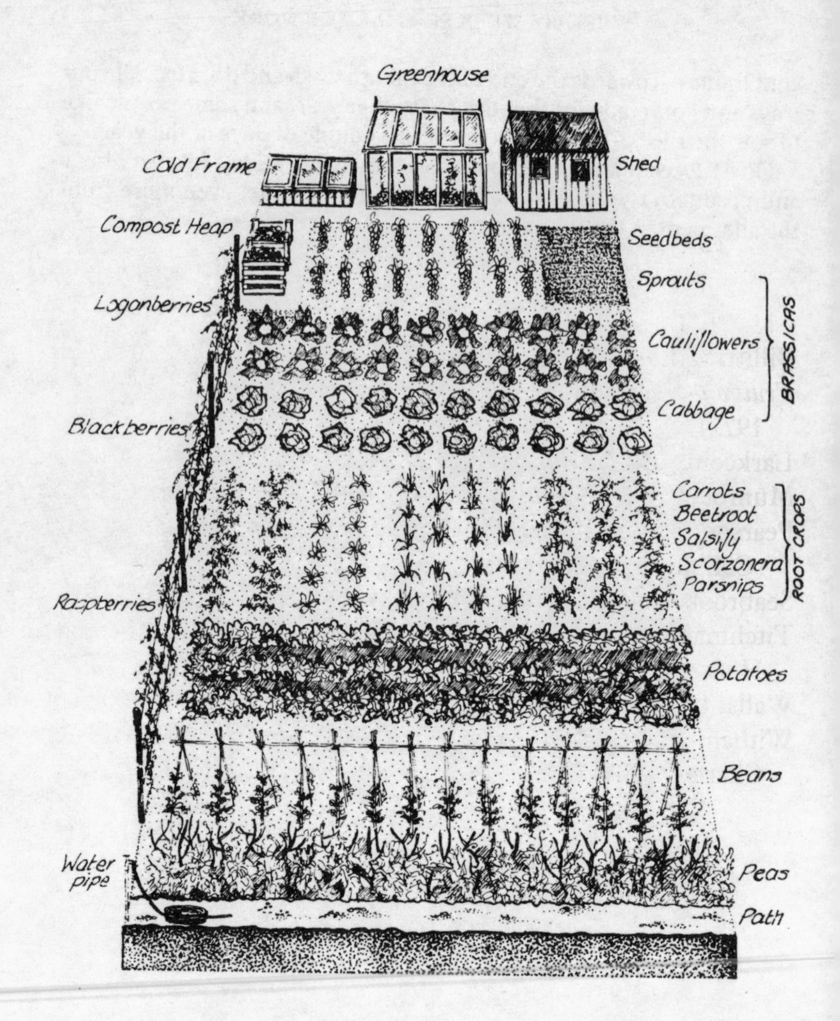
Greenhouse
Cold Frame
Shed
Compost Heap
Seedbeds
Sprouts
Loganberries
Cauliflowers
BRASSICAS
Cabbage
Blackberries
Carrots
Beetroot
Salsify
Scorzonera
Parsnips
ROOT CROPS
Raspberries
Potatoes
Beans
Water pipe
Peas
Path

Further reading

Billitts, Arthur. *ABC of Vegetable Growing* (Hamlyn, 1981)
Fruit and Vegetable Gardener's Handbook (Marshall Cavendish, 1977)
Larkcom, Joy. *Salads the Year Round* (Hamlyn, 1980)
Munroe, C.J. *The Smallholder's Guide* (David & Charles, 1979)
Pearson, Robert (ed). *The Wisley Book of Gardening* (Collinbridge, 1981)
Seabrook, Peter. *Complete Vegetable Gardener* (Cassell, 1976)
Titchmarsh, Alan. *The Allotment Gardener's Handbook* (Severn House, 1983)
Walls, I.G. *Tomato Growing Today* (David & Charles, 1977)
Witham Fogg, H.G. *Salad Crops All Year Round* (David & Charles, 1983)

Index

Page numbers in **bold** type refer to illustrations.